WORLD BANK WORKING PAPER NO. 217

Youth Employment and Skills Development in The Gambia

Nathalie Lahire
Richard Johanson
Ryoko Tomita Wilcox

THE WORLD BANK
Washington, D.C.

ISBN: 978-0-8213-8811-2
eISBN: 978-0-8213-8813-6
ISSN: 1726-5878

DOI: 10.1596/978-0-8213-8811-2

Library of Congress Cataloging-in-Publication Data

Youth employment and skills development in The Gambia / [prepared by Nathalie Lahire].
      p. cm.
   "This report was prepared by Nathalie Lahire and included the following team members: Priscilla Elms, Ryoko Wilcox, and Richard Johanson."
   Includes bibliographical references.
   ISBN 978-0-8213-8811-2 -- ISBN 978-0-8213-8813-6
   1. Vocational education--Gambia. 2. Technical education--Gambia. 3. Youth--Employment Gambia. 4. Youth--Gambia--Social conditions. 5. Gambia--Economic conditions--1965- I. Lahire, Nathalie.
   LC1047.G3Y68 2011
   370.113096651--dc22

                                                                               2011018726

Contents

Boxes

Figures

Tables

Acknowledgments

This report was prepared by Nathalie Lahire and included the following team members: Priscilla Elms, Ryoko Tomita Wilcox, Vicente Garcia Moreno, and Richard Johanson. Support, advice and comments were also provided by Peter Materu, McDonald Benjamin, George Afeti (Secretary General of the Commonwealth Association of Polytechnics in Africa), Margo Hoftijzer, Fadilla Caillaud, and Peter Darvas. Rose-Claire Pakabomba provided valuable administrative support. Peer reviewers were Carlos Cavalcanti, Ganesh Rasagam, and Tazeen Fasih.

This report, financed by the Norwegian Post Basic Education Fund (NPEF), is also the product of close collaboration between the Understanding Children's Work (UCW), The Gambia Bureau of Statistics (GBOS), UNDP, the National Training Authority, the Ministry of Basic and Secondary Education and the World Bank. The report benefited from the results of a new survey carried out by the GBOS and referred to as The Gambia Joint Rural Labor Force /CDDP Baseline Survey), which was co-financed by NPEF, UNDP, and the World Bank CDDP project. The study also benefited from a background paper prepared by UCW informing chapters two and three. The team wishes to extend special thanks to the Ministry of Trade, Regional Integration, and Employment and especially Mrs. Naffie Barry, Permanent Secretary, for her support in organizing the workshop at which the results of this study were presented and for facilitating the rich discussion. The team is also grateful to the Gambian youth who were the true inspiration for this study. Finally, the team gives thanks to Barnaby Rooke for his excellent editing work.

Acronyms and Abbreviations

CBO	Community Based Organization
CDDP	Community Driven Development Project
CPI	Consumer Price Index
DTIS	Diagnostic Trade Integration Study
EC	European Commission
ECOWAS	Economic Community of West African States
EFA-FTI	Education for All Fast Track Initiative
GDP	Gross Domestic Product
GSQF	The Gambia Skills Qualifications Framework
GTTI	The Gambia Technical Training Institute
HIPC	Highly Indebted Poor Countries
ICA	Investment Climate Assessment
ICT	Information Communication and Technology
ILO	International Labour Organization
LMIS	Labor Market Information System
NATC	Njawara Agricultural Training Center
NGO	Non Governmental Organization
NPEF	Norwegian Post Basic Education Fund
NTA	National Training Authority
NYSS	National Youth Service Scheme
PRSP	Poverty Reduction Strategy Paper
RY	Reference Year
QNIT	Quantum Net Institute of Technology
TVET	Technical and Vocational Education and Training
UNDP	United Nations Development Program

CURRENCY EQUIVALENTS

(Exchange Rate Effective June 5, 2010)

Currency Unit = Dalasi (D)

US$1 = D 26.75

FISCAL YEAR

January 1–December 31

Vice President:	Obiageli Ezekwesili
Country Manager/Director:	Habib Fetini
Sector Manager:	Christopher J. Thomas
Task Team Leader:	Nathalie Lahire

Executive Summary[1]

Why Focus on Youth Employment and Skills Development in The Gambia?

Despite substantial improvements in access to basic education and steady economic growth, The Gambia still faces considerable challenges in respect to reducing poverty. As the result of its narrow economic base and its reduced internal market, the country will continue to rely heavily on the productivity of its citizens to reverse the cycle that keeps families in poverty generation after generation. Poverty reduction is a complex equation that involves improvements in job creation, especially for high-skilled and productive employment, as well as improvements in human capital levels to ensure that citizens are able to take advantage of employment opportunities. Currently, however, low human capital levels greatly limit the productivity and employment outcomes of the population, as evidenced by the fact that a majority continues to work in subsistence agriculture, especially in rural areas.

Nearly 60 percent of the poor in The Gambia are under the age of 20 years. Youth face significant challenges with respect to employment outcomes, such as a very difficult transition from school to work and very low levels of education and training. In terms of education levels, a significant proportion of young people (especially in rural areas) leave school early, in part due to what are perceived to be low returns on education. Many of those who do receive high quality education and training choose to emigrate. In a country where more than half the population is under the age of 20 years, these trends are worrisome.

The second Poverty Reduction Strategy Paper II (2007-2015, PRSP II) recognizes the need to focus on improving youth employment outcomes. It states that "The Gambia has a problem of youth unemployment especially those that have limited skills. Consequently, a big proportion of the youth are part of the people categorized as poor in The Gambia. PRSP II will focus on the problem of youth unemployment through various approaches including supporting private sector investment that creates jobs for the youth, increasing access to productive assets particularly credit by the youth, and retooling and training the youth to increase their employability."

How Do Youth in The Gambia Spend Their Time?

Youth (defined as the group aged 15 to 24 years) is a time of significant transition throughout the world and The Gambia is no exception. Most youth face one of several paths. If they are in school, they may: (i) continue their schooling, possibly combining school and work, or (ii) leave school for the workplace. Those who never attended school may: (i) find employment, or (ii) continue to work, for those that had to enter the labor market at an early age. The latter two options offer limited prospects for young people with no formal education and limited human capital.

The evidence suggests that youth in The Gambia display a very difficult transition from school to employment. School attendance decreases substantially between 15 and 19 years, but reduced enrollment is not accompanied by a similar increase in employment, meaning that many students drop out of school to become inactive. Young people in rural areas leave school earlier than young people in urban areas. Some 73 percent of the 15 to 17 years age group in urban areas is still in school, against 61 percent in rural areas.

Young people living in cities and towns are much more likely to be unemployed than their rural counterparts. This again underscores the different nature of urban and rural economies, and in particular the important role that the agriculture sector plays in absorbing young rural workers. Young people are more likely than adults to be unemployed or jobless. The picture does however vary according to the area of residence. Rural unemployment is low and varies little across the whole age spectrum, predominantly as a result of these workers being absorbed into the agricultural sector. Urban unemployment peaks for young adults, aged 20 to 24 years.

Overall, young workers are employed in jobs of low quality and high levels of informality. Female youth are also much more likely to be self-employed (46 percent, versus 32 percent for male youth). More than half of young workers are engaged in agriculture, which predominates in rural areas (82 percent, versus 16 percent in urban areas), and the services sector is the most important source of youth employment in cities and towns, accounting for almost 65 percent of employed youth. Female youth are less likely to be employed or in education, and more likely to be inactive (31 percent, against 27 percent for male youth); possibly reflecting the period when child-rearing and domestic responsibilities begin for female youth.

What Determines Youth's Employment Outcomes?

The study assessed the impact of the following factors on youth's time use: education level, gender, local labor supply and demand, and place of residence. From the analysis, it was noted that the probability of being employed decreases as the level of human capital increases. In fact, uneducated youth display the highest probability of being employed. However, with respect to the quality of the employment, the following should be noted:

- Higher levels of household income in rural areas are associated with lower youth employment than in urban areas;
- Female youth are 8 percent less likely to be employed. The gender difference is more pronounced for youth with primary and secondary education, for whom the gender gap increases to 10 percent;
- The impacts of both young people's gender and level of education on the probability of being employed are much higher in rural areas than in urban areas; and
- The impact of the local labor supply on the probability of youth employment is not statistically significant; however, local labor demand appears to substantially influence the probability of finding employment regardless of the level of education.

In terms of education levels, most youth have very little opportunity to acquire human capital. Over 50 percent reached primary education at best, 26 percent reached upper basic education, and 18 percent reached senior secondary or higher education. Low human capital is a particular concern in rural areas given that formal education is much more limited than in urban areas. In rural areas, half of young people have no education at all. This group of young people that never reach school or leave early is a particular policy concern. It is worth noting, however, that the proportion of those with no schooling was lower for teenagers than for young adults in rural and urban areas alike, pointing to progress over time in expanding access to basic education. Descriptive evidence suggests that better educated young people may in fact face greater difficulty in securing jobs, but that the quality of the jobs they eventually do find is better.

Children's Involvement in Employment

As many youth in The Gambia leave school and/or start work at an early age, it is necessary to examine how children (defined as the group aged seven to 14 years) spend their time and the determinants of this time use.

Children's employment is an overwhelmingly rural phenomenon, mainly attributable to the agriculture sector. Urban children are much more likely to attend school without working (66 percent, compared with 33 percent for rural children). The 23 percent of urban children who are in employment are most likely to work in the services sector (retail trade, etc.) Whereas rural children are most likely to work on the family farm, urban children are more likely to work as paid employees or in self-employment outside the confines of the family.

For this age group, school attendance peaks at 12 years, when almost 88 percent of children are in school. After this however, school attendance drops and inactivity rises as children begin to leave school to seek full-time work. The age of 12 years is therefore when parents and children make important decisions about pursuing education.

The Determinants of Children's Time Use

The study assessed the impact of the following factors on children's time use: gender, household income, household composition, the gender and level of education of the household head, and place of residence. Analysis of the survey data highlights the following important points about the factors determining how children spend their time:

- Boys are more likely to be in employment;
- Children from larger households are more likely to be idle, or not combine school and work;
- Twice the level of household income carries a higher probability of combining school and work, but does not significantly affect the chances of only attending school;
- Children from households whose head is male are more likely to be in employment;
- The level of parents' education has a strong positive impact on their children's education level and time spent in school; and
- The likelihood of attending school and being in employment varies significantly by place of residence. For instance, children from Basse (the most remote region) display the highest probability of only working and the lowest probability of only attending school. Urban children are more likely to just attend school, and less likely to combine school and work.

Provision of Technical and Vocational Education and Training

TVET provision consists of several dimensions, including pre employment training provided by government institutions, NGOs and private training bodies. Public institutions tend to offer postsecondary training, and are mainly concentrated in Banjul. The premier public institution is the Gambia Technical Training Institute (GTTI) which provides certificate and diploma courses at the postsecondary level and is mandated to train middle-level manpower in commerce, business, accounting, engineering, and construction. Enterprise based training is a major source of skills acquisition for those in work, both paid employment and in the informal sector. The majority of private training institutions offer certificate and diploma courses in commerce, management, accounting, finance, and IT. Nongovernmental organizations (NGOs) and community based organizations (CBOs) mainly provide training to low-income individuals. The traditional apprenticeship system is also a major source of skills acquisition for those in employment, especially male youth in the informal sector. However parents often arrange for their male children to be apprenticed to master craftsmen in roadside workshops where the quality of this training is usually low. Training tends to cover traditional production such as metalwork, vehicle maintenance, carpentry, furniture making, and so on.

Public provision of skills training. There are just nine public training centers: the GTTI, mainly financed by student tuition fees, the Hotel School; the Gambia College (for agriculture), the Rural Skills Training Center at Mansa Konko, the Julangel Skills Training Center, the Kotu in-house Training Center, the President's Award Scheme Training Center, the Gambia Telecommunications and Multimedia Institute; and the Management Development Institute.

The National Youth Service Scheme (NYSS) also provides training for youth. However a tracer study conducted by UNDP found that as high as 57 percent of the program's graduates were unemployed and that the program was not cost effective.

Private provision of skills training. Currently, there are approximately 15 NGOs and CBOs providing skills training. In comparison to public and private for profit training, the output of nonprofit providers is low. They mainly focus on low-income students and those with basic or no education. About 45 private for-profit training institutions operate at present.

No regulated system of apprenticeship exists in the formal sector. However, enterprises do provide in-house training when skills are lacking. According to the National Training Authority Enterprise Training Needs Assessment Survey of 2007, most skills are acquired on the job. About 61 percent of surveyed companies provided in-service training to their workers.

TVET Financing

Although current estimates of public TVET expenditure are not available, evidence from earlier years suggests that TVET accounted for less than four percent recurrent education expenditure. This share is likely to have decreased substantially as spending on basic education has taken priority and enrollments in basic and secondary education have increased. Government subsidies for the GTTI have certainly decreased substantially. In addition, there have been few capital investments in TVET over the years by the government or by donors. According to data from 2006, salaries accounted for 86 percent of spending and nonsalary inputs for nearly 14 percent. However, it appears that the bulk of TVET financing comes from non government sources (only a minority of TVET institutions are government owned and run). One distinguishing feature of TVET in The Gambia is the willingness of parents and trainees to pay for training.

Strengths and Weaknesses of TVET

The 2002 TVET Policy, the PRSP II, and the National Education Policy provide the framework for TVET planning. Recent reforms of the sector have focused on developing a labor market information system, establishing a training levy, developing standards and qualifications (including a skills qualification framework and assessment, certification and accreditation processes), and creating the National Training Authority (NTA).

An analysis of the current structure of the TVET sector was conducted for this study, considering external efficiency (economic and social relevance), effectiveness, the quality of training provision, organization and management effectiveness, internal efficiency, resource mobilization and utilization, and sustainability. According to these criteria, the main strengths are the existence of a sound policy and strategic framework, and the existence of a key organization, the NTA, to spearhead reforms. The NTA is helping to raise both the relevance and quality of the system through market analysis; the definition of occupational competencies, with employer's help; the registration and accreditation of training providers, and the development of a body of assessors. Additional strengths include the GTTI, which has a long tradition of skills provision; extensive NGO and CBO provision of TVET; a widespread system of informal apprenticeships; and the willingness of parents and trainees to pay for training.

The main challenges are the inadequate financing of TVET, including an unsustainable levy system; the lack of tracer studies on labor market outcomes; inadequate opportunities for access to training by youth; inadequate coverage in priority areas (such as horticulture); the lack of management information about TVET; disparities in the quality of provision; and insufficient entrepreneurship training. In addition, the NTA does not have a streamlined system of accreditation, a management information system on training, or the capacity to support training institutions in curriculum development. Neither does it have appropriate financing to implement its programs. Lastly, the GTTI appears to be relatively isolated from employers and the labor market.

Recommendations for Policy Makers

Define a better fiscal and monetary policy mix. Specific recommended actions include enforcing a hard budget constraint on the operations of state owned enterprises and reducing unnecessary government spending.

Pursue economic policies that stimulate the creation and growth of enterprises and hence the demand for employable skills. Training, even of the highest quality, is not enough to generate employment. Rather, it is the growth of enterprises that creates additional skills needs and opportunities for new jobs. Therefore, the economic policy dimension should not be overlooked.

Provide an enabling environment for business innovation and growth to stimulate demand for relevant skills training. Given that the best opportunity for job creation comes from business start-ups, actions to lower the costs of starting and running businesses would have a high payoff. These actions include: (i) establishing a transparent business environment that is free of undue privileges; (ii) simplifying the tax system; and (iii) setting high standards in public administration services.

Encourage foreign companies to contribute to national skills development efforts. Foreign companies operating in the country can contribute to the development of human capital in the country through the technology transfer process. The government should encourage foreign companies to train local workers and establish partnerships with local training institutions.

Conduct more in-depth research to better understand how children's employment affects schooling and youth employment outcomes. Remedial education programs and other "second chance" opportunities for children in employment are important measures in overcoming work related damage to children's welfare. Programming experience elsewhere points to three main options to offer disadvantaged, unenrolled children opportunities to return to school: (i) mainstreaming, or providing returning children and working children with special remedial support within the regular classroom context; (ii) school based catch-up education, involving separate, intensive courses making use of school facilities; and (iii) nonformal bridging education, involving intensive courses designed to raise academic proficiency.

Correct the levy system, as a matter of urgency. The previous levy system prompted strong resistance from some sectors, such as banking. The current system penalizes small merchants. Putting the TVET system on a sound financial footing is a top priority. A study of alternatives and the advantages and feasibility of each should be conducted urgently.

Develop a strategy to raise the quality of traditional apprenticeships. Traditional apprenticeship is probably the principal means through which male youth acquire skills. The NTA has developed an apprenticeship policy; now a strategy including objectives, resources and actions must be developed to raise the quality of traditional apprenticeships.

Develop a specific strategy for the acquisition of skills by female youth. Traditional apprenticeship mostly excludes female youth. They may also be neglected by artisan level training It is clear that young women tend to be placed in traditional occupations with low income generating potential. Consequently, more analysis is needed to identify potential occupations (demand constraints) and the nature and extent of the underprovision of training to female youth (supply constraints) in order to determine appropriate remedies.

TVET Level Recommendations

Intensify partnerships between training providers and employers. Partnerships can take the form of joint skills training programs, use of part-time industry based experts as key advisors and instructors, and access to modern factory equipment by learners in pre employment training programs. Innovative partnerships between training institutions and the private sector can lead to greater relevance, quality, and cost-effectiveness in training delivery.

Continuously update the professional and pedagogical skills of TVET instructors and system managers. This should enable them to respond to the challenge of designing new training programs and strengthening existing ones.

Increase the use of technology and modern farm practices in the agricultural sector. The agricultural sector employs the largest number of workers. However, the sector still operates at the subsistence level, and its productivity is declining. Modern farm practices and technology can help increase productivity and the demand for employable skills in areas such as food preservation and agro-processing, maintenance and repair of farm machinery, and the fabrication of simple agricultural tools. Extending technology to rural areas can also contribute to stemming the rural to urban migration.

Take globalization into account in skills development strategies. The process of globalization and liberalization of international markets can undermine the competitiveness of indigenous goods and services, even on the domestic market. Skills development strategies should therefore target productive sectors where the country has a competitive advantage.

Incorporate a life-long learning element in skills development strategies. Learning critical skills such as creative thinking, problem-solving and team-work is a prerequisite for reskilling, upskilling and multiskilling. Systems for the validation of prior learning, and national skills qualification frameworks also encourage life-long learning. The NTA should therefore be supported to complete its work in progress on the Gambia Skills Qualification Framework.

Include an environmental sustainability component in skills development programs. Occupational areas such as refrigeration and air-conditioning, automobile repair and servicing, mining and oil exploration can have adverse effects on the environment. Training providers should be sensitized on the environmental risks associated with the practice of such occupations and include them in their training programs.

Provide counseling services prior to and in parallel with youth skills development programs. Youth skills development programs preceded by adequate counseling of potential trainees often have greater impact and higher chances of success for trainees, and enhance their employability. This is important given that employability is the key goal of training.

Emphasize gender, equity, and access dimensions in training. Access to skills development programs not only has a gender bias but also economic and geographical biases. Youth from poor households and rural backgrounds and female youth in particular should therefore receive financial support to acquire productive skills for employment.

Strengthen and streamline the NTA. The National Training Authority is the lynchpin of TVET reform, and is particularly well suited to provide coherence and direction to the dispersed non government training providers that prevail. The NTA needs to be further strengthened and made sustainable in the following areas:

- Revitalize the Skills Development Fund to support the achievement of NTA policy objectives and priorities;
- Build the highly valuable labor market information system. This will enable: (i) tracer studies for institutions; and (ii) local market analysis for training centers, particularly in rural areas;
- Operationalize the Gambia Skills Qualifications Framework (GSQF) to harmonize standards among the informal and formal sectors;
- Simplify licensing and accreditation requirements, focusing on basic minimum standards at the initial licensing stage. Accreditation requirements can then stress quality assurance processes; and
- Ensure that the NTA is financially sustainable and receives the recurrent financing it needs to carry out its seminal functions. Also, caution and restraint should be exercised in scaling up the GSQF. Existing occupational profiles should be fully developed, tested and revised before developing new occupational standards.

Assist the GTTI in raising the quality and relevance of its training. The GTTI has a continuing lead role to play in the delivery of technical and vocational skills, but it needs additional investment. However, the following activities should first be undertaken:

- Conduct an academic audit of the GTTI;
- Build its management information system;
- Build better links between the GTTI and employers;
- The GTTI should consider partnerships with private training providers to avoid duplicating training in low-cost fields, and concentrate on areas that private providers are not willing to cover (high-cost technical fields); and
- Invest in curricula development, new and replacement equipment, and especially in-service staff development.

Review and strengthen NYSS performance by learning from successful youth training and employment schemes in Africa. The following actions could be undertaken:

- Include Banjul and more female trainees in the NYSS;
- Rely on rigorous market analysis and tracer studies (by the NTA);
- Include multiskilling;
- Pay serious attention to entrepreneurship training;
- Provide placement assistance, microcredit and mentoring; and
- Avoid establishing an NYSS multipurpose training center; instead, rely on other training providers, but make financing conditional on performance.

Recommendations for Employers

Provide more labor market information. The efficiency of the formal labor market depends on the availability of vacancy information, which is scarce in The Gambia. The use of informal social networks to identify candidates may negatively affect the matching of labor supply and demand as they do not guarantee that the information collected is neutral and truthfully reflects job seekers' actual skills. However, given that most jobs are found through social networks, it is worth considering how to help youth tap into networks to which they might not necessarily have access, especially higher skilled youth in urban areas.

Give young people information on skills in demand and sectors that will experience growth in the future. This will enable them to make informed decisions about skills training opportunities.

Areas for Further Study

While this study focuses primarily on documenting situation of youth in The Gambia, and the correlation between labor and education status, a further study is needed to assess how the outcomes presented are the result of the country's poorly functioning labor market. This should be a multisector effort analyzing the private sector, macroeconomics, and human development.

Notes

1. General Note: for the purpose of this study, the following definitions of age groups are used: 'teenagers' are aged 15 to 19 years; 'young adults' are aged 20 to 24 years; and 'adults' are aged 25 to 55 years. 'Youth' comprise the first two categories.

CHAPTER 1

Introduction

It's time for policy makers now to look beyond the silos, to begin recognizing that consistent, cost-effective investment in children and youth can pay for itself. Providing young people with the resources they need to compete in today's global economy is not just a moral imperative. It is an economic necessity, too.

— James J. Heckman, Nobel Laureate in Economics

Objectives of the Study

Despite substantial improvements in access to basic education and steady economic growth since 2003, The Gambia still faces considerable challenges with respect to reducing poverty. As the second Poverty Reduction Strategy Paper notes, reverting the rising poverty trend continues to be a challenge. Despite relatively steady economic growth, 58 percent of the population continues to live in poverty. Youth are particularly affected: nearly 60 percent of the poor in The Gambia are under the age of 20. Moreover, youth face significant challenges with respect to employment: the transition from school to work is very difficult and levels of education and training are very low. These challenges are reflected in the significant proportion of young people who are neither in employment or following education or training. Moreover, when youth do find employment, it is usually of poor quality. In terms of education, a significant proportion of young people (especially in rural areas) leave school early, in part because the return on education is perceived to be low. Many of those who do receive high quality education and training choose to emigrate. In a country where more than half the population is under the age of 20, these trends are worrisome.

This report has been elaborated in response to a request from the Gambian government, who is keen for the World Bank and other donors to get involved in the area of skills' development and postprimary education. The report provides groundbreaking information and analysis which can help the government in making informed decisions in relation to how education and skills' development can improve employability and productivity.

The report's primary audience and stakeholders are several Gambian ministries, including the Ministries of Basic, Secondary, and Higher Education, the Ministry of Youth and Sports, and the Ministry of Trade and Employment. Other interested parties include the National Training Authority, the private sector, World Bank, other development partners, and training institutions.

The report aims to gain a better understanding of youth employment outcomes in the hope of crafting more sound and responsive policies to address the related trends. The first part of this study provides an analysis of how youth spend their time and the determinants of this time use. This is of interest because young people tend to abandon school for the workplace at an increasingly early age, if they attend school at all. Micro data from the 2008 Gambia Joint Labor Force/CDDP Baseline Survey and from the 2002/2003 Integrated Household Survey are examined.

The Gambian government recognizes that one of the main ways of enhancing young people's skills is through technical and vocational education and training. In order to improve youth employability, it will be necessary for the government to improve the quality of teaching and learning in adult, nonformal and continuing education as well as in formal education. A coherent strategy to improve Gambians' education and skill set will require a multipronged approach that not only provides quality education to the traditional formal school system users, but will also address the needs of functionally illiterate adults and nonenrolled youth.

Thus, the second part of the study provides an overview and analysis of the technical and vocational education and training sector. It also provides recommendations on how the sector can be made more responsive to the needs of youth in the light of the findings of the first part of the study.

Methodology

The data used to undertake the analysis and develop the specific policy recommendations in this report was provided by a 2008 household survey financed under the Norwegian Post Basic Education Fund, in collaboration with the World Bank Community Driven Development Project and UNDP, referred to as the Joint Rural Labor Force/CDDP Baseline Survey.[1] Other data sources include The Gambia Integrated Household Survey on Consumption Expenditure (IHS, 2003), the Poverty Level Assessment (2002/03) and the Investment Climate Assessment survey (2006).

Socio-Economic Context and Education Trends

The Gambia is a small West African country with an estimated population of 1.6 million, average GDP per capita of US$320, and a Human Development Index ranking of 155 out of 177 countries in 2007.

The health sector has been under great pressure over the years, attributable to a number of factors, namely: a high demographic growth rate, inadequate financial and logistic support, the shortage of adequate and appropriately trained health staff, a high staff attrition rate, and the lack of an efficient and effective referral system. These factors have seriously constrained efforts to reduce morbidity and mortality rates in the country.

The links between economic growth and the level of education are well understood (the impact on growth of externalities generated by improved education levels, such as better adaptability, easier learning-by-doing for example). There is strong evidence that the cognitive skills of the population are powerfully related to individual earnings, to the distribution of income, and to economic growth. New empirical results show the importance of both minimal and high-level skills, the complementarity of skills and the quality of economic institutions, and the robustness of the relationship between skills and growth (Hanushek and Woessmann, 2007). Improved education can be seen as the single factor of the growth process that most contributes to increase the intrinsic quality and productivity of both labor and capital (Bosworth and Collins, 2003).

The education system has made significant progress over the past years. The growth in upper basic (grades 7 to 9) and senior secondary (grades 10 to 12)[2] has been accompanied by important developments in private sector participation and household cost-sharing. Upper basic students pay their registration fees and senior secondary students pay their school fees,[3] although waivers are available to students from poor households. Despite these improvements, the access to higher grades is constrained by the limited number of schools, especially at the secondary level.

Macroeconomic Trends

After falling into a severe crisis in the mid 1980s and early 1990s, The Gambia succeeded in reversing the economic downturn. Economic progress has been made since 1997, and the foundations for sustainable growth laid. Between 1997 and 2001 real GDP has witnessed steady growth, at approximately six percent per year, and inflation has been low. Despite these improvements, exogenous risks such as erratic rainfall, the decline in trade, and regional instability are not negligible. In 2002, real GDP declined by three percent, mainly because of the drought and loss of agricultural production. The fiscal deficit worsened in the same year, further destabilizing the economy. This reflects another key risk, that of shocks attributable to the inconsistent implementation of sound macroeconomic policies and inadequate governance. In 2003, fiscal and monetary policies were tightened, assuring the resumption of growth, lowering inflation, and stabilizing of other macro conditions. The Gambia's macroeconomic performance has shown continued improvement in recent years in large part due to fiscal and monetary discipline. Nonetheless, growth is currently slowing because of the global recession. The annual real GDP growth rate has averaged 6.2 percent in the last five years, compared with an estimated annual population growth rate of approximately 2.8 percent. However, real GDP growth is believed to have dropped to five percent in 2009 because of the impact of the global financial crisis (see Table 1.1).

Table 1.1: Macroeconomic Trends, by Key Indicators, 2006-2009 (percent)

	2006	2007	2008	2009 (Estimation)
Real GDP Growth	6.5	6.3	6.1	5.0
Current Account Balance (% GDP) Including Official Transfers	13.4	12.3	16.0	14.6
Foreign Assistance (% of GDP) Official Transfers	1.3	1.2	1.2	3.4
Remittances (% of GDP)	10.2	8.1	6.6	5.9
CPI Inflation (per year)	2.1	5.4	4.5	4.5

The economy is relatively undiversified and limited by a small internal market. Services account for over half of GDP, reflecting the importance of external trade and tourism. Tourism is a key driver of the economy and the country's most significant foreign exchange earner followed by reexports and groundnut production (see Table 1.2). Agriculture accounts for approximately 33 percent of GDP and more than 70 percent of employment. Unlike some countries in West Africa, The Gambia does not have abundant natural resources, thus making it even more reliant on the productivity of its labor force to generate revenues.

Table 1.2: Main Exports of The Gambia, by Sector (millions of US$)

Sector (most recent date)	Gross Foreign Exchange Earnings	Net Foreign Exchange Earnings
Tourism (2005)	100.0	54.6
Reexports (2004-05)	137.0	20.0
Groundnut Products (2004-06)	12.0	10.0
Cashew Nuts (2005/06)	1.9	1.7
Fruit and Vegetables (2003-05)	0.9	0.8
Sesame Seeds (2003-05)	0.6	0.5
Fish Products (2003-05)	0.5	0.4
Total	252.9	88.0

Source: Joint World Bank and African Development Country Assistance Strategy (2008).

Sectoral Growth Rates

Sectoral growth rates indicate that agriculture has experienced the highest average per capita growth since 2003, by far. The industry and services sectors grew at similar per capita rates, both lower than the real GDP per capita average growth rate. Nevertheless, all three major sectors have experienced fairly strong per capita real growth since 2003. Industry registered the highest employment growth rate, largely thanks to the construction sector which grew more rapidly than any other subsector, at almost twice the national average.

Since 2003, agriculture accounts for the livelihood of 50 percent of the working population and 63 percent of the poor, which is significantly more than industry and services. Therefore, the sector's growth performance will have a proportionately larger impact on overall growth and poverty reduction. In rural areas, 80 percent of the population, an overwhelming majority, works in agriculture (Poverty assessment, 2009). Groundnuts are the country's main cash crop although exports have declined drastically since the 1980s.

The Gambia's longer term policy objectives for economic growth are detailed in the ambitious Vision 2020 document which aims to transform the country into "…a tourist paradise, a trading export oriented agricultural and manufacturing nation, thriving on free market policies and a vibrant private sector…".[4] Tourism has attracted a lot of investment, with net foreign exchange earnings estimated at US$50 million, after deducting imported inputs and other payments abroad. This is larger than all other exports combined.

The Diagnostic Trade Integration Study (DTIS) report estimates that hotels generate more than 4,000 jobs, or 2,700 equivalent full-time jobs; to this, a similar amount of direct employment in restaurants, excursions, taxis, and shops can be added, and another 3,000 indirect jobs with suppliers (DTIS, 2008). Jobs in tourism are also relatively well remunerated. The average monthly earnings of a hotel worker, including tips, have been estimated at between D 30,000 and D 50,000 (US$1,115 to US$1,858) and these estimates are only for a half-year job.[5] Rough estimates from the DTIS suggest that feasible growth in cashew exports over the next ten years could offer income to some 30,000 households, generating annual revenues almost twice as high as for groundnut farmers.

The DTIS also notes that fishing, horticulture, sesame seeds, and cashew nuts are promising areas for export diversification.

Poverty Profile

Poverty Head Count by Age Groups

Estimated poverty ratios by age groups indicate that poverty in The Gambia has a distinctly youthful characteristic. Nearly 60 percent of the poor are under the age of 20, which reflects a bottom-heavy population pyramid resulting from relatively high birth rates and rapid population growth (see Table 1.3). The country's estimated birth rate is 38 per 1,000 inhabitants, higher than the world average of 21 per 1,000 inhabitants, but in line with the average for least developed countries of 36 per 1,000 inhabitants and the West African average of 42 per 1,000 inhabitants (Poverty Assessment, 2009). The estimated poverty rates by age groups indicate that the youngest (those aged less than 15 years) have relatively high poverty rates. The group aged more than 49 years also has a relatively high incidence of poverty, but accounts for a small percentage of the population.

According to the poverty assessment, the urban youth unemployment rate is very high, at 22 percent, compared with the national unemployment rate of six percent, and the rural youth unemployment rate of three percent.

Table 1.3: Poverty Rates and Distribution, by Age Groups, 2009 (percent)

	Poverty Headcount Rate	Distribution of the Poor	Distribution of the Population
0-5	63.8	17.5	15.9
6-14	62.1	27.5	25.7
15-19	55.2	11.7	12.3
20-24	55.5	9.6	10.0
25-29	51.3	7.7	8.8
30-34	50.2	5.6	6.5
35-39	52.1	4.5	5.1
40-44	54.3	3.8	4.0
45-49	53.1	2.8	3.0
50-54	58.6	2.4	2.3
55-59	61.2	1.6	1.5
60-64	58.6	1.7	1.7
65+	65.0	3.5	3.2
Average/Total	56	100	100

Source: 2003 IHS and authors' calculations on the basis of Poverty Assessment, 2009 data.

Poverty by Sector of Employment

According to the economic census conducted in June 2005, poverty is substantially higher for households working in the agriculture and fishing industries, with 76.4 percent classified as poor compared with 46.2 percent on average for other households.

Table 1.4: Poverty Rate of Household Heads, by Sector of Employment, 2003 (percent)

Industry	Share Living Below the Poverty Line
Agriculture and Fishing	76.4
Manufacturing and Energy	50.0
Construction	63.6
Trade, Hotels and Restaurants	48.8
Transport and Communication	52.4
Private and Public Financial Administration	49.2
Social Services	45.4
Not Stated	53.5
Overall Average	57.9

Agricultural and fishing households account for over half the population living in extreme poverty (see Table 1.4). Poverty is lower amongst those working in the social services, public and private financial services, trade, hotels and restaurants.

Intra-Sectoral and Rural-Urban Migration

The recently completed Poverty Assessment (2009) indicates that Gambians are migrating out of the agriculture sector into industry and services. In particular, the education, transport, communication, hotels, and restaurants subsectors grew the fastest. The growth of the education sector most probably reflects the government expansion of the public school system.

The rural to urban migration has been even more striking (see Table 1.5). The Poverty Assessment stated that over the past 15 years, the economically active population in urban areas grew by an average annual rate of 4.65 percent compared with 1.29 percent in rural areas. The intra-sectoral shifts in the population are primarily attributable to the migration away from rural areas and towards cities, especially by those working in agriculture. The migration into industry and services (construction, transport and communication, hotels and restaurants and education) reflects the internal migration into urban areas and out of agriculture (Poverty Assessment, 2009).

Table 1.5: Intra-Sectoral and Rural-Urban Migration (annual percentage change)

	Urban	Rural	Total
Agriculture and Fishing	7.07	1.60	2.26
Manufacturing and Energy	3.90	0.11	2.51
Construction	6.69	1.86	4.85
Trade, Hotels, Restaurants	4.39	-0.66	2.97
Transport and Communication	5.07	0.24	3.55
Other Services	4.00	0.40	2.91
National	4.65	1.29	2.62

Source: Poverty Assessment (2009).

International Migration

What sets The Gambia apart from other countries in the region is the significantly higher emigration rate of those having completed higher education, estimated at 65 percent, compared with 24 percent for Senegal, 43 percent for Ghana, 41 percent for Sierra Leone, and 3.3 percent for Burkina Faso. According to the recent poverty assessment, the emigration rate of the highly educated is among the top 15 countries in the world. As a result of the large number of Gambians working abroad, remittances constitute a large percentage of revenues.

However some macro econometric studies find that the threshold emigration rate above which the brain drain becomes harmful for development can be prudently estimated at between 15 and 20 percent in low-income countries.[6] The average optimal emigration rate (which maximizes country gains) probably lies between 5 and 10 percent. In 2009, total remittances are expected to sharply decline by approximately 20 percent to 5.6 percent of GDP and 3.4 percent of total per capita consumption, as a result of the global recession.

Notes

1. A detailed note on the computation method used to obtain a representative sample can be found in Appendix A.
2. Upper basic and senior secondary are commonly known in the sector as lower and upper secondary.
3. Registration fees are paid once per student and per school. School fees are annual enrollment fees.
4. Diagnostic Trade Integration Study (DTIS, 2008).
5. Mitchell and Faal, 2008.
6. Studies reviewed in Docquier, 2006.

CHAPTER 2

Overview of Youth Employment and Training

Introduction

The 15 to 24 years life period is a time of significant transition for young people throughout the world and Gambian youth are no different. Most of them face one of several paths. If they are in school, they may: (i) continue their schooling, possibly combining school and work, or (ii) leave school for the workplace. Those who never attended school may: (i) find employment, or (ii) continue to work, for those that had to enter the labor market at an early age. The latter two options offer limited prospects for young people with no formal education and limited human capital. The next section will take a closer look at youth involvement in the labor market and provide an analysis of the determinants of youth employment.

This chapter provides the profile of how young people spend their time in The Gambia. Besides low employment rates, young people are disadvantaged in many other ways: a significant proportion are neither in employment nor in education or training; an equally significant proportion (especially in rural areas) leave school early, partly as the result of education's perceived low returns; and the quality of employment among young workers is low.

The definition of youth includes individuals aged 15 to 24 years. This study also provides an analysis of two subgroups: those aged 15-19 years (teenagers) and those aged 20-24 years (young adults). This enables the distinction between youth in and out of the secondary school age range. While most teenagers are expected to be in school rather than working, the opposite occurs with young adults. As such, these two groups are likely to display different employment outcomes, especially concerning labor force participation, inactivity and unemployment rates.

Youth Involvement in the Labor Market

Time Use among Young People

Gambian youth comprise both students and workers. The table below, which differentiates between five unique activity categories, indicates that 25 percent of young people are in full-time work and two percent are not attending school and are looking actively for work. Thirty-five percent are still in full-time education or training. Given that work and schooling are not necessarily mutually exclusive, an additional nine percent combine the two. The low percentage of youth involved in both activities suggests that, in the Gambian context, these two activities are not very complementary. A large group of young people (29 percent) are inactive, meaning that they are neither in the labor force nor in education (see Table 2.1). This category might also include discouraged workers (those who are no longer looking for work) as well as people with disabilities (see Box 2.1 on terminology).

Table 2.1: Youth Employment Status, by Age Group, 2008 (percent)

Age Group	Unique Activity Categories						Aggregate Activity Categories		
	Only in Work (1)	Only in Education (2)	Combining Work and Education (3)	Unemployed and not Attending School (4)	Inactive (5)	Total	Employed (1) and (3)	In Education (2) and (3)	Jobless and not Attending School (4) and (5)
15-17	14.1	53.6	14.0	0.2	18.0	100	28.1	67.6	18.2
18-19	20.7	40.8	11.3	1.4	25.8	100	32.0	52.1	27.2
20-24	34.0	18.3	5.1	4.4	38.3	100	39.1	23.4	42.7
Total	24.5	34.8	9.4	2.3	28.9	100	33.9	44.2	31.2

Source: UCW calculations based on The Gambia Joint Rural Labour Force/CDDP Baseline Survey, 2008.

Age

The aggregates presented above mask large variations in how young people spend their time by age. This is not surprising as the 15 to 24 years age range is a period of transition from adolescence to adulthood and from education to working life. School attendance declines rapidly with age. Comparing teenagers and young adults, there are large differences in education enrollment, with comparatively few (23 percent) continuing education beyond their teens. Young adults (both employed and unemployed) tend to be

---

Box 2.1: Youth Labor Market Outcome Terminology

Employed Person	A person who fulfils any of the following criteria: (i) he/she worked for a person or business, for a salary, cash or pay in kind, (ii) he/she was self-employed, (iii) he/she worked for the family without compensation, (iv) he/she worked for someone else without compensation, or (v) he/she is going to start a new business/job or return to work. This definition excludes chores for one's own household.
Unemployed Person	A person who fulfils all of the following criteria: he/she is without work, and he/she has been actively seeking employment in the course of the past month.
Inactive Person	A person who is neither employed, unemployed or in education.
Joblessness	The sum of unemployed and inactive people.

more highly represented in the labor force, and among the inactive group. This also suggests that youth in The Gambia face a very difficult transition from school to employment. School attendance decreases substantially between 15 and 19 years, but reduced enrollment is not accompanied by a similar increase in employment, meaning that many students drop out of school to become inactive. The combination of part-time work and schooling is not uncommon among 15 to 17 year-olds (14 percent), but declines among subsequent cohorts. Only five percent of young adults combine the two activities.

Gender

Gender considerations appear to have an impact on how young people spend their time. Overall, young ladies are less likely to be employed than their male counterparts (32 percent, versus 36 percent) or to be in education (42 percent, versus 46 percent). Indeed, 29 percent of male youth falls into this category, whereas it accounts for 33 percent of female youth. These figures might reflect the different gender based social roles that young people take on as they enter adulthood. This is the period when child-rearing and domestic responsibilities begin for female youth and when male youth become economically productive.

Residence

The time use profiles of young people are strongly affected by underlying differences in the rural and urban labor markets (see Table 2.2). Urban youth benefit from greater education opportunities, staying in school longer and joining the labor force later. They are more likely to be in education than their peers in rural areas (47 percent versus 40 percent). Some 73 percent of 15 to 17 years age group in urban areas is still in school, against 61 percent in rural areas. For young adults, the figures fall to 24 percent and 22 percent, respectively.

Leaving school early in rural areas might have several explanations. The opportunity cost of work may be higher in rural areas given that subsistence agriculture is predominant and labor intensive, and families who own land need their family members to work on it. Rural youth are much more likely to be employed than their urban counterparts (51 percent versus 24 percent) as a result. Rural youth are able to provide labor on the family farm without the need for a lengthy job search or formal contractual arrangements.

Youth Unemployment and Joblessness

The measured unemployment rates are relatively low among Gambian young people. Eight percent of the active youth are unemployed (that is, they report having searched for a job in the past month). Joblessness, arguably a better measure of the youth employment disadvantage because it also captures discouraged workers, is higher. Some 29 percent of male youth and 34 percent of female youth are jobless. It is worth mentioning that unemployment and joblessness are lowest for the 15 to 17 years age group (see Table 2.3).

Table 2.2: Youth Employment Status, by Age Group, Gender and Residence, 2008 (percent)

	Age Group	Unique Activity Categories						Aggregate Activity Categories		
		Only in Work (1)	Only in Education (2)	Combining Work and Education (3)	Unemployed and not Attending School (4)	Inactive (5)	Total	Employed (1) and (3)	In Education (2) and (3)	Jobless and not Attending School (4) and (5)
Male	15-17	15.9	52.3	16.8	0.0	15.0	100	32.7	69.1	15.0
	18-19	20.1	41.0	13.4	2.0	23.4	100	33.5	54.4	25.4
	20-24	32.7	20.9	6.4	3.7	36.1	100	39.1	27.3	39.8
	Total	24.6	35.2	11.2	2.2	26.7	100	35.8	46.4	28.9
Female	15-17	12.6	54.7	11.7	0.4	20.5	100	24.3	66.4	20.9
	18-19	21.3	40.6	9.2	0.8	28.1	100	30.5	49.8	28.9
	20-24	35.2	15.6	3.7	5.0	40.4	100	38.9	19.3	45.4
	Total	24.4	34.5	7.7	2.5	30.9	100	32.1	42.2	33.4
Urban	15-17	6.1	62.3	10.2	0.2	21.2	100	16.3	72.5	21.4
	18-19	13.0	47.9	8.6	1.9	28.5	100	21.6	56.5	30.4
	20-24	26.1	19.9	4.2	5.6	44.2	100	30.3	24.1	49.8
	Total	16.8	39.6	7.1	3.1	33.4	100	23.9	46.7	36.5
Rural	15-17	26.0	40.8	19.7	0.2	13.3	100	45.7	60.5	13.5
	18-19	36.1	26.6	16.5	0.5	20.3	100	52.6	43.1	20.8
	20-24	47.9	15.5	6.6	2.1	27.8	100	54.5	22.1	29.9
	Total	37.7	26.8	13.3	1.1	21.1	100	51.0	40.1	22.2

Source: UCW calculations based on The Gambia Joint Rural Labor Force/CDDP Baseline Survey, 2008.

Table 2.3: Youth Unemployment Characteristics, by Age Group, 2008 (percent)

Age Group	Unemployed to Population Ratio[a]	Unemployment Rate[b]	Inactivity	Joblessness
15–17	0.9	3.0	18.0	18.9
18–19	1.6	4.8	25.8	27.4
20–24	4.8	10.8	38.3	43.1
15–24	2.8	7.6	28.9	31.7

Source: UCW calculations based on The Gambia Joint Rural Labour Force/CDDP Baseline Survey, 2008
Note: (a) The unemployment ratio is the total unemployed of an age group expressed as a proportion of the total population of that group.
(b) The unemployment rate refers to the total unemployed of an age group as a proportion of the total workforce of that group.

Young people living in cities and towns are much more likely to be unemployed than their rural counterparts. The urban unemployment rate is 13 percent, compared with two percent in rural areas. This again underscores the different nature of urban and rural economies, and in particular the important role that the agriculture sector plays in absorbing young rural workers (see Table 2.4).

Table 2.4: Youth Unemployment Characteristics, by Age Group, Gender and Residence, 2008 (percent)

	Age Group	Unemployed to Population Ratio[a]	Unemployment Rate[b]	Inactivity	Joblessness
Male	15–17	0.3	1.0	15.0	15.3
	18–19	2.1	5.9	23.4	25.5
	20–24	4.3	9.8	36.1	40.4
	Total	2.6	6.6	26.7	29.3
Female	15–17	1.3	5.2	20.5	21.8
	18–19	1.1	3.6	28.1	29.2
	20–24	5.2	11.7	40.4	45.6
	Total	3.0	8.5	30.9	33.9
Urban	15–17	1.3	7.3	21.2	22.5
	18–19	2.2	9.0	28.5	30.7
	20–24	6.2	16.8	44.2	50.4
	Total	3.7	13.3	33.4	37.1
Rural	15–17	0.2	0.5	13.3	13.5
	18–19	0.5	0.9	20.3	20.8
	20–24	2.3	4.0	27.8	30.1
	Total	1.2	2.3	21.1	22.3

Source: UCW calculations based on The Gambia Joint Rural Labour Force/CDDP Baseline Survey, 2008
Note: (a) The unemployment ratio is the total unemployed of an age group expressed as a proportion of the total population of that group.
(b) The unemployment rate refers to the total unemployed of an age group as a proportion of the total workforce of that group.

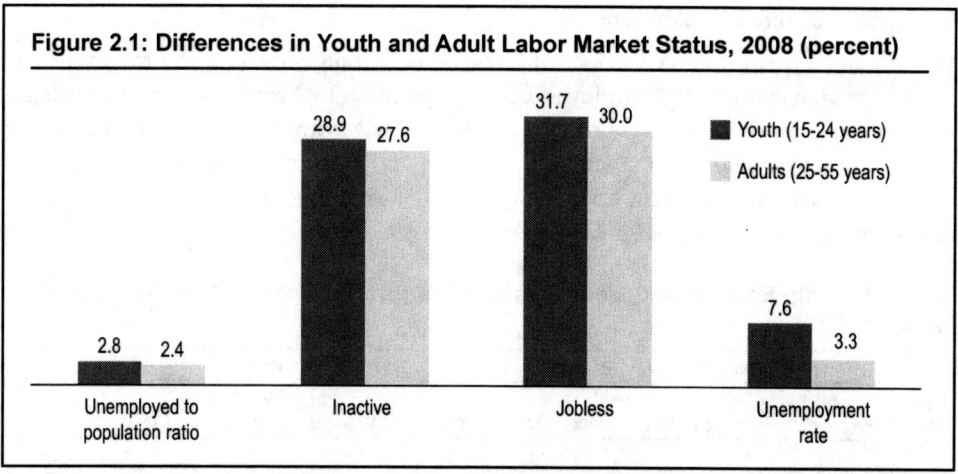

Figure 2.1: Differences in Youth and Adult Labor Market Status, 2008 (percent)

Source: UCW calculations based on The Gambia Joint Rural Labour Force/CDDP Baseline Survey, 2008.

Comparison of Youth and Adult Labor Market Outcomes

Comparing youth and adult unemployment rates provides an indication of the extent to which young workers are disadvantaged in relation to adults in securing jobs (see Figure 2.1). Young people are more likely than adults to be unemployed (expressed as a percentage of the labor force) or jobless.

The picture does however vary according to the area of residence (see Figure 2.2). Rural youth appear to face less difficulty in securing employment; the rural unemployment rate is low and varies little across the whole age spectrum. This is predominantly a result of these workers being absorbed into the agricultural sector and does not reflect the quality of employment.

However, this is not the case for youth living in cities and towns. The urban unemployment rate peaks for young adults, but is also high among 25 to 29 years age group. This illustrates that in many cases the period required to settle into work extends well into adulthood. It is worth noting that there is no information about the number of hours worked.

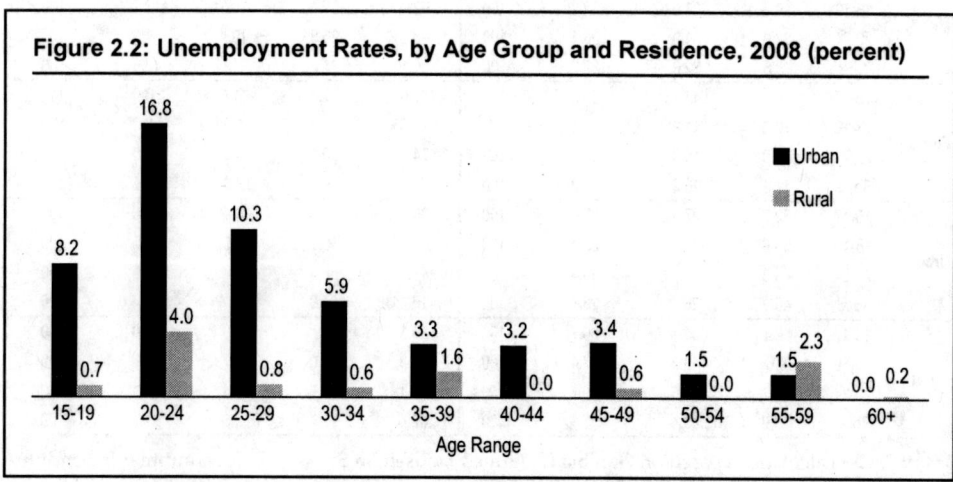

Figure 2.2: Unemployment Rates, by Age Group and Residence, 2008 (percent)

Source: UCW calculations based on The Gambia Joint Rural Labour Force/CDDP Baseline Survey, 2008.

Composition of Youth Employment[1]

Young workers are employed in jobs of low quality and high levels of informality. Table 2.5, which breaks down the employed youth population by broad occupational categories, indicates that young people's jobs are distributed primarily across unpaid family work (41 percent), self-employment (39 percent) and paid employment (20 percent). Age appears to play a role in occupational choices: unpaid family work decreases in importance with age, whereas paid employment increases.

Table 2.5: Youth Employment Modalities and Sector of Activity, by Age Group, 2002 (percent)

Age Group	Modality of Employment				Sector of Activity				
	Paid Employee	Self-Employed	Unpaid Family Work	Total	Agri-culture	Services	Manufac-turing	Other	Total
15-17	8.4	34.0	57.7	100	81.1	14.8	4.1	0.0	100
18-19	20.8	36.7	42.5	100	73.7	22.8	2.8	0.8	100
20-24	23.8	41.3	35.0	100	59.9	29.3	7.8	3.0	100
Total	20.2	39.1	40.7	100	66.4	25.3	6.2	2.0	100

Source: UCW calculations based on The Gambia Integrated Household Survey on Consumption Expenditure and Poverty Level Assessment, 2002/03.
Note: The "Other" category includes construction, electricity, gas and water industries.

These aggregates mask large differences between the rural and urban youth labor markets, and between male and female youth (see Table 2.6). Paid employment is preponderate in cities and towns (49 percent, versus 11 percent in rural areas) and among male youth (29 percent, versus 12 percent for female youth), whereas unpaid family work is relatively more common in rural areas (46 percent, versus 26 percent in urban

Table 2.6: Youth Employment Modalities and Sector of Activity, by Age Group, Gender and Residence, 2002 (percent)

	Age Group	Modality of Employment				Sector of Activity				
		Paid Employee	Self-Employed	Unpaid Family Work	Total	Agri-culture	Services	Manufac-turing	Other	Total
Male	15-17	11.0	24.3	64.8	100	82.3	12.0	5.7	0.0	100
	18-19	39.2	27.6	33.2	100	63.7	29.4	4.7	2.2	100
	20-24	32.0	34.9	33.1	100	48.2	36.8	10.4	4.6	100
	Total	28.8	32.0	39.2	100	56.5	31.2	8.8	3.4	100
Female	15-17	5.9	43.2	50.8	100	80.0	17.4	2.7	0.0	100
	18-19	10.3	41.9	47.8	100	78.8	19.3	1.9	0.0	100
	20-24	14.0	48.8	37.2	100	74.3	20.1	4.6	1.0	100
	Total	11.6	46.2	42.2	100	76.5	19.4	3.6	0.6	100
Urban	15-17	32.7	27.4	39.9	100	39.7	49.1	11.2	0.0	100
	18-19	66.8	9.8	23.4	100	22.2	70.3	7.5	0.0	100
	20-24	48.3	28.3	23.4	100	11.5	66.4	16.2	5.9	100
	Total	48.9	25.8	25.4	100	16.4	64.8	14.4	4.4	100
Rural	15-17	4.2	35.1	60.7	100	88.3	8.8	2.9	0.0	100
	18-19	9.6	43.2	47.1	100	86.3	11.0	1.7	0.9	100
	20-24	13.7	46.6	39.7	100	79.1	14.7	4.4	1.8	100
	Total	10.9	43.4	45.7	100	82.4	12.7	3.6	1.2	100

Source: UCW calculations based on Gambia Integrated Household Survey on Consumption Expenditure and Poverty Level Assessment, 2002/03.
Note: The "Other" category includes construction, electricity, gas and water industries.

areas) and among female youth (43 percent, versus 39 percent for male youth). Female youth are also much more likely to be self-employed (46 percent, versus 32 percent for male youth). This may be because self-employment is a strategy to overcome poverty, particularly for women, and is an alternative to unemployment.

The agriculture sector absorbs the largest proportion of the labor force, including youth. More than 65 percent of employed youth is engaged in agriculture, followed by 25 percent in services and six percent in manufacturing. Again, however, differences by residence are large. While agriculture not surprisingly predominates in rural areas (82 percent, versus 16 percent in urban areas), the services sector is the most important source of youth employment in cities and towns, accounting for almost 65 percent of employed youth. The composition of employment also varies by gender and the age of the worker. Female youth are more commonly found in agricultural work than their male counterparts, and conversely male youth are more likely to be involved in the services sector. There appears to be a shift toward the services sector and manufacturing from the agricultural sector as individuals grow older (see Table 2.7).

For the sake of comparison, this study includes the analysis of other groups, namely adults of working age (25 to 55 years). Differences in terms of work characteristics between youth and adults of working age provide one indication of the youth labor market disadvantage. The composition of youth and adult employment differs in urban areas as well as in rural areas. In both, the largest difference is the greater involvement of young people in unpaid family work and agriculture. Young workers are also less likely to be involved in paid work and services than their older counterparts. Adult workers, on the other hand, are much more likely to be self-employed.

Table 2.7: Youth and Adult Employment Modalities and Sector of Activity, by Residence, 2002 (percent)

	Age Group	Modality of Employment				Sector of Activity				
		Paid Employee	Self-Employed	Unpaid Family Work	Total	Agri-culture	Services	Manufac-turing	Other	Total
Total	15–24	20.2	39.1	40.7	100	66.4	25.3	6.2	2.0	100
	25 -55	29.7	50.8	19.5	100	48.6	42.3	4.7	4.4	100
Urban	15–24	48.9	25.8	25.4	100	16.4	64.8	14.4	4.4	100
	25 -55	52.3	36.1	11.7	100	10.1	76.7	7.7	5.5	100
Rural	15–24	10.9	43.4	45.7	100	82.4	12.7	3.6	1.2	100
	25–55	18.1	58.5	23.5	100	66.7	26.1	3.4	3.9	100

Source: UCW calculations based on Gambia Integrated Household Survey on Consumption Expenditure and Poverty Level Assessment, 2002/03.

Note: The "Other" category includes construction, electricity, gas and water industries.

Determinants of Youth Employment Outcomes

Determinants of Youth Employment

In this section, we present econometric evidence of the impact on youth's time use and employment, of socio-demographic factors, local labor market characteristics, and access to school. The analysis is based on the 2008 Gambia Joint Rural Labor Force/CDDP Baseline Survey.

Simple regression tools permit an exploration of the correlation between human capital and youths' labor market outcomes. We have followed the approach applied in Guarcello et al. (2006), which attempts to identify whether the effects of a set of youth's labor market outcomes' explanatory variables are different according to the level of education reached by the individual. While this approach does not directly answer the question of the causal effect of human capital on employability,[2] it might offer some indirect evidence. We have therefore divided the sample according to the level of education achieved. In particular, we have considered three groups: no schooling, primary education, and secondary and higher education. For each of these subsamples, we have run a separate regression on the employment probability.

There is an obvious sample selection problem, presumably because youth with higher levels of education are not a random sample and their latent level of labor supply and demand for schooling are likely to be correlated with unobservable characteristics. One option to deal with this issue would be to elaborate a selection model and follow a generalized procedure (such as Heckman's (Heckman, 1979). However, there are potential costs to this approach. Sometimes, the bias in the coefficients can be worse than in the naïve model, and an instrument appropriate for education is hard to find. We hence warn the reader that the resulting estimates have to be interpreted with some care.

Education Level

The probability of being employed decreases as the level of human capital increases. Uneducated youth display the highest probability of being employed (12 percent higher than youth with primary education, and 20 percent higher than those with secondary or higher education). This difference illustrates the close and inverse correlation between the decision to participate in the labor market and that of investing in human capital (see Appendix Tables B.1 to B.3). In addition, it might reflect the fact that youth with lower education and skill levels have no other choice but to be employed in order to survive. Youth with higher education levels might come from wealthier households and can therefore afford to remain unemployed for longer while they continue their job search.

Gender

The results show that the effect of gender is large. On average, the probability of being employed is eight percent lower for female youth. The gender difference is more pronounced for youth with primary and secondary education (see Appendix Tables B.4 and B.5). Female youth with primary and secondary education are over 10 percent less likely to work than their male counterparts. At the same time, for youth with low levels of human capital (that is without education) and for youth with high levels of human capital (that is with higher education) the gender effect on the probability of being employed is not significant.

Household Characteristics

Household characteristics, and in particular the level of spending, appear to affect the probability of employment. Twice the level of household spending is associated with a three percent drop in youth employment for the entire sample. The impact of household spending on youth employment is highest for those with secondary education. Even if this result should be taken with care, it seems to indicate that credit rationing and parental resources are important determinants of the youth employment probability.

Local Labor Supply and Demand

Two indicators were used to assess the links between the local labor market conditions and youth employment outcomes: (i) the prime age (25 to 55 years) employment to population ratio, an indicator of aggregate local labor demand; and (ii) the youth to prime age population ratio, an indicator of aggregate local labor supply. Both these indicators are computed for each local government area, and disaggregated according to urban and rural residence.

The conditions of local labor demand appear to substantially influence the probability of finding employment for young people, regardless of their level of human capital. A 10 percent increase in labor demand increases probability of being employed by 20 percent for uneducated youth, by 29 percent for youth with primary education and by 20 percent for youth with secondary or higher education. The impact of local labor supply on the probability of youth employment is not statistically significant for any of the subsamples. In other words, an increase in the proportion of the young population does not appear to have an impact on their employment outcomes.

Place of Residence

The effect of the place of residence is also significant for employment prospects: the probability of employment for rural youth is eight percent higher than for their urban counterparts, although this largely reflects the fact that many rural youth work on the family farm. The impacts of the area of residence on the probability of being employed are highest for youth with secondary education.

To better reflect the large differences according to the place of residence, we have estimated the equations for rural and urban areas separately. It is important to note that as the result of the disaggregation of youth by area of residence and education level, the subsamples are small and the estimates are statistically unrepresentative and should be interpreted with particular care. The impacts of both gender and human capital on the probability of being employed are much higher in rural areas than in urban areas.

Econometric evidence (see Appendix Tables B.1 to B.3) confirms the importance of household income in explaining youth employment patterns in rural areas. Higher household income in rural areas is associated with lower youth employment than in urban areas. Surprisingly, access to piped water has a larger impact on the probability of youth employment in urban areas than in rural areas. Access to piped water might also capture some other effects as this variable could be a proxy for socio-economic status.

Higher local labor demand increases the probability of finding employment for both urban and rural youth regardless of their human capital. The effect is more than twice as noticeable for rural youth with primary, secondary and higher education, than for their urban counterparts. On the other hand, the impact of labor demand on the probability of employment for urban uneducated youth is higher than for rural uneducated youth. The impact of youth labor supply is not significant in urban areas.

Incidence of Training

The data in this section are drawn from the Investment Climate Assessment (ICA; World Bank, 2009). The assessment relies partly on the results of an enterprise survey undertaken in 2007.[3] A sample of 174 formal companies and 127 informal urban companies was surveyed in the Greater Banjul Area. The survey includes a sample of 122 employees of which 20.5 percent are young people, and 81 percent are male. Although the sample size is small, the survey provides some initial clues about the incidence of training among young people. It contains detailed data on their marital status, wages, education level, citizenship status, training received and its duration, job level, relationship to the firm's owner, health status during the last month, and number of working hours. More specifically in relation to training, the survey asks about the exact training the respondent followed in both current and past jobs.

Table 2.8 presents the characteristics of this sample. The reader is asked to interpret this analysis with care given the small sample of employees in the ICA survey.

Table 2.8: Social, Professional, and Education Characteristics of 122 Workers, for Youth and Adult Workers, 2006

	Variable	Entire Sample	Young Workers	Adult Workers
Professional Profile	Monthly Wages (Dalasis)	8,123	18,047	5,807
	Log Wages (%) (a)	10.4	10.6	10.3
	Workload (Hours per Year)	2,725	2,846	2,694
	Employed by a Family Member (%)	17.2	32	13.4
	Experience (Years)	8.7	3.2	10.1
	Tenure in Current Position (Years)	4.5	2.4	5
	Union Member (%)	19.8	0	23.6
Socio-Demographic Profile	Male (%)	81.14	60	86.6
	Aged 15 to 24 Years (%)	20.5	100.0	0
	Aged More than 24 Years (%)	79.5	0	100.0
	Married (%)	54.1	8	66.0
	Healthy (%)	32.8	44	29.9
	Expatriates (%)	7.44	8	7.3
Education Profile	Schooling Completed (Years)	7.4	10.2	6.6
	Not Educated (%)	23.0	12	25.8
	Primary Level (%)	8.2	4	9.3
	Upper Basic Level (%)	30.3	12	35.0
	Senior Secondary Level (%)	29.5	56	22.7
	Higher Level (%)	9.0	16	7.2
Training Profile	Trained (%)	27.9	16	30.9
	Training Received (months)	31.5	1.7	35.5
Job Profile	Management (%)	1.89	0	2.3
	Professionals (%)	19.81	0	23.6
	Skilled Production Workers (%)	49.06	65	46.1
	Unskilled Production Workers (%)	26.41	29	25.8
	Non Production Workers (%)	2.83	6	2.2
Sample Size		122	25	97

Source: Analysis based on ICA data (2006)

Note: Log wages is the mathematical transformation of the wages variable by logarithm. This enables the interpretation of the regression model results in terms of a percentage variation. In this instance, log wages show the average percentage increase in wages by year of training.

Young workers have 10.2 years of schooling on average, and as such are more educated than adult workers, with 7.4 years. The majority of young workers has senior secondary education whereas adult workers have only completed upper basic, or are not educated. Young workers have less job experience, are not union members, have received less training, are mainly skilled production workers, and are more likely to be related to the firm's owner (an average of 32 percent are a family member). Young workers are the healthiest and tend to work more than adults.

Out of the 25 young employees, only 16 percent received some form of professional training compared with 31 percent of adults. The mainly self-financed professional training was completed by the young workers before beginning their current job. Fifty six percent of young workers reported having attained the senior secondary level of education (see Table 2.9). Only eight percent of them benefited from professional training within the firm.

Table 2.9: Incidence of Training among Young Workers, by Education Level, 2006 (percent)

Education Level	Training		Total
	No	Yes	
None	12	0	12
Primary	12	4	16
Senior Secondary	44	8	52
Technical Secondary	12	0	12
Vocational Training	0	4	4
University Degree	4	0	4
Total	**84**	**16**	**100**

Source: Analysis based on ICA data (2006).
Note: Chi (2) = 6.8; Pr=0.2

Analysis of the Incidence of Training

We have used the Probit model (see Table 2.10) to identify the determinants of training in the private sector. The results show that by combining young and adult workers in a pooled sample using the same ICA database, the probability of receiving training is highly and positively correlated to education and experience (at a five percent level of significance). Adult workers are more likely to receive training than young workers (at a 10 percent level of significance). According to the results, gender and marital status have no influence on the incidence of training for either group. For young workers, the most educated and those with more experience are more likely to receive training. The same patterns are observed for adult workers.

Table 2.10: Correlation between Various Worker Characteristics and Training, According to the Probit Model, for Youth and Adult Workers, 2006 (correlation coefficients)

	Variable	Entire Sample	Young Workers	Adult Workers
Professional Profile	Workload	..	..	..
	Employed by a Family Member	..	..	..
	Experience	0.10 (3.01)	0.26 (2.01)	0.048 (2.07)
	Tenure in Current Position	-0.11 (-1.84)	..	..
	Union Member	0.36 (0.82)	..	..
Socio-Demographic Profile	Male	-0.23 (-0.48)	..	..
	Aged 15 to 24 Years	-1.17 (-1.91)	..	..
	Married	-0.37 (-0.98)	..	..
	Healthy	..	..	..
	Expatriates	..	..	..
Education Profile	Schooling Completed	0.19 (3.96)	0.22 (1.21)	0.18 (3.76)
Job Profile	Professionals	..	..	0.98 (2.69)
	Skilled Production Workers	-0.47 (-1.11)	..	..
	Unskilled Production Workers	..	..	..
	Non Production Workers	..	..	..
Constant		-1.93 (-2.68)	-4.52 (-1.87)	-2.73 (-4.39)
Statistical Data	Number of Observations	106	25	89
	Log likelihood	-42.32	-7.35	-39.31
	LR chi2	37.75	7.28	28.91
	Prob>chi2	0.0000	0.0262	0.0000
	Pseudo R-Squared	0.31	0.33	0.27
Sample Size	122	25	97	

Source: Analysis based on ICA data (2006)
Note: All figures are presented at a 10% level of significance, except in between brackets, at a 5% level of significance.
.. indicates that the correlation is not significant.

Training and Wage Premium

The Jacob Mincer equation (see Table 2.11), which provides an estimation of the impact of schooling on earnings (see Mincer, 1974), shows an upward trend in wage profiles as schooling, experience, and training increase. The wage return associated with training is positive and significant (at a five percent level of significance). The equation also reveals that there is no difference in the wage returns related to education, experience and training, between young and adult workers.

Table 2.11: Correlation between Various Worker Characteristics and Wage Return, According to the Jacob Mincer Equation, 2006 (correlation coefficients)

	Variable	Entire Sample
	Workload	0.0002 (2.09)
	Employed by a Family Member	..
Professional Profile	Experience	0.04 (3.85)
	Tenure in Current Position	..
	Union Member	..
	Male	-0.38 (-1.78)
	Aged 15 to 24 Years	-2.49 (-0.48)
Socio-Demographic Profile	Married	0.74 (4.15)
	Healthy	0.41 (1.92)
	Expatriates	..
Education Profile	Schooling Completed	0.14 (5.03)
Training Profile	Training Received	0.005 (2.14)
	Management	..
	Professionals	..
Job Profile	Skilled Production Workers	..
	Unskilled Production Workers	..
	Non Production Workers	..
	Schooling	0.11 (0.30)
Young Workers Only	Experience	0.01 (0.10)
	Training Received	0.34 (0.59)
Constant	7.51 (13.03)	
	Number of Observations	34
Statistical Data	Fstat	4.96
	Prob>F	0.0007
	R-Squared	0.71
Sample Size	122	

Source: Analysis based on ICA data (2006)
Note: All figures are presented at a 10% level of significance, except in between brackets, at a 5% level of significance.
.. indicates that the correlation is not significant.

Human Capital Levels and Youth Labor Market Outcomes

This section examines the role of human capital accumulation in relation to the labor market outcomes for young people. Most youth have very little opportunity to acquire human capital. Over 50 percent reached primary education at best, 26 percent reached upper basic education, and 18 percent reached senior secondary or higher education (see Table 2.12).

Table 2.12: School Attainment Levels, by Residence and Age Group, 2002

	Highest Education Level Attained	Urban		Rural		Total	
		Number	%	Number	%	Number	%
15-19	No Schooling	11,181	21.5	37,689	37.9	48,870	32.3
	Primary	8,996	17.3	24,547	24.7	33,542	22.1
	Upper Basic	21,193	40.8	29,614	29.8	50,807	33.5
	Secondary and Higher	10,578	20.4	7,699	7.7	18,277	12.1
20-24	No Schooling	16,433	33.1	39,853	56.4	56,285	46.8
	Primary	6,020	12.1	7,117	10.1	13,137	10.9
	Upper Basic	10,010	20.1	10,936	15.5	20,946	17.4
	Secondary and Higher	17,253	34.7	12,726	18.0	29,978	24.9
Total	No Schooling	27,614	27.2	77,541	45.6	105,155	38.7
	Primary	15,016	14.8	31,663	18.6	46,679	17.2
	Upper Basic	31,203	30.7	40,550	23.8	71,753	26.4
	Secondary and Higher	27,830	27.4	20,425	12.0	48,255	17.8

Source: UCW calculations based on The Gambia Integrated Household Survey on Consumption Expenditure and Poverty Level Assessment, 2002/03.

Low human capital is a particular concern in rural areas given that formal education is much more limited than in urban areas. In rural areas, half of young people have no education at all. The proportion of those with no schooling was lower for teenagers than for young adults in rural and urban areas alike, pointing to progress over time in expanding access to basic level schooling.

This group of school nonentrants and early-leavers is a particular policy concern; they are especially vulnerable to undesirable employment outcomes because of their limited human capital. Unenrolled children are most vulnerable to child labor, which cannot be separated from the issue of finding satisfactory employment as adults. However, it should be noted that in the absence of information on past employment, it is not possible to estimate the precise proportion of young people that were working as children.

Descriptive evidence suggests that better educated young people may in fact face greater difficulty in securing jobs, but that the quality of the jobs they eventually do find is better. Figure 2.3 shows employment and unemployment rates by level of education. It shows that the rate of unemployment increases with the level of education, peaking among those with higher education. This is partially the product of the fact that less educated young people are available to work at an earlier age, and therefore have greater exposure to the labor market and more time to secure employment. In addition, as the reservation wage[4] is likely to rise with skill levels, the time spent searching for work may increase with an individual's level of human capital. As such, this finding therefore says little about the relation of human capital to success in the labor market.

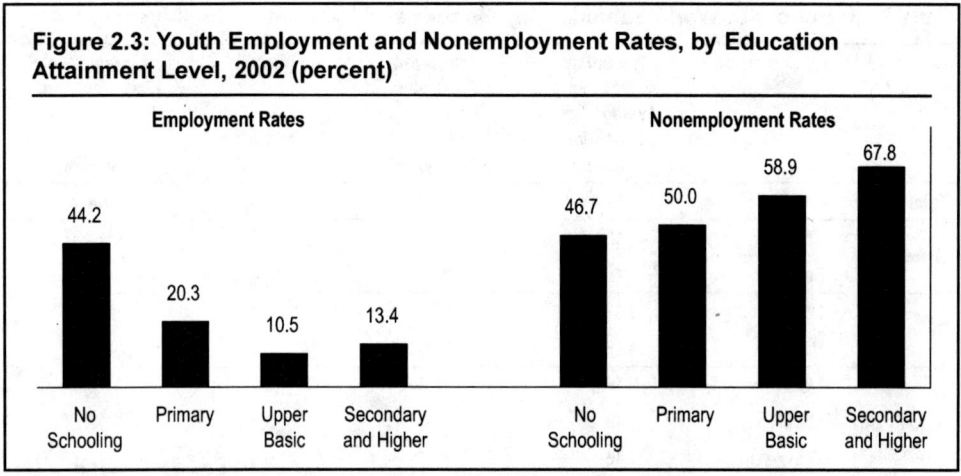

Figure 2.3: Youth Employment and Nonemployment Rates, by Education Attainment Level, 2002 (percent)

Source: UCW calculations based on The Gambia Integrated Household Survey on Consumption Expenditure and Poverty Level Assessment, 2002/03.
Note: An individual is nonemployed if he/she is not working and defines his/her main occupation as being unemployed.

Figure 2.4 shows the distribution of young adults by type of occupation and level of education. It shows that the most educated workers are much more likely to be in paid employment and much less likely to be in unpaid work than their less educated counterparts.

School-to-Work Transition

Neither the 2003 nor the 2008 household survey data provided conclusive evidence as to the school-to-work transition. The study therefore refers to data from 1998. Table 2.13 presents information on the transition from school to work. The average age of those who drop out of school represents the starting point of the transition, whereas the average age of those starting work for the first time represents the end. The third column

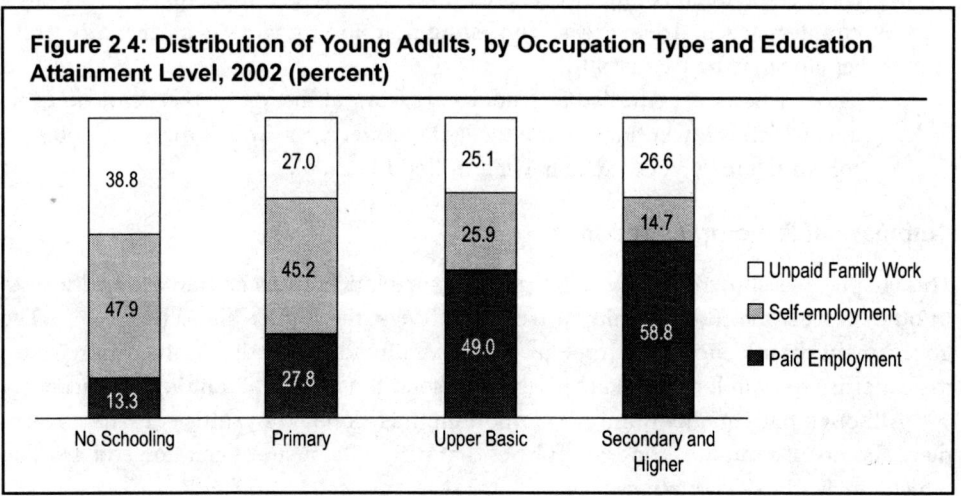

Figure 2.4: Distribution of Young Adults, by Occupation Type and Education Attainment Level, 2002 (percent)

Source: UCW calculations based on Gambia Integrated Household Survey on Consumption Expenditure and Poverty Level Assessment, 2002/03.

Table 2.13: School to Work Transition, by Gender and Residence, 1998 (years)

		Transition Start Point: Average Age of School Drop-outs	Transition End Point: Average Age of First Employment	Transition Period	Average Age of First Employment for Children who Never Attended School*
Total		17.4	23.2	5.8	14.4
Gender	Male	18.6	23.7	5.1	15.5
	Female	16.1	20.7	4.6	13.6
Residence	Urban	17.7	24.5	6.8	17.5
	Rural	16.5	20.0	3.5	13.9
Gender and Residence	Male/Urban	18.6	24.8	6.2	18.6
	Male/Rural	18.2	21.6	3.4	15.2
	Female/Urban	16.8	23.4	6.6	15.2
	Female/Rural	14.8	17.4	2.6	12.9

Source: UCW calculations based on National Household Poverty Survey, 1998; and *Gambia Joint Rural Labour Force/CDDP Baseline Survey, 2008.*

shows the duration of the transition, highlighting the difficulties that young people face in entering the labor market. The last column illustrates when youth who never attended school start work.

From Table 2.13, the following facts are worth noting:

■ Male youth spend longer in education, thus possessing a higher likelihood of reaching higher education, than their female counterparts. Hence, male youth start the transition to work at a later age than females, in both urban and rural areas;

■ The transition starts later in urban than in rural areas for both male and female youth, suggesting that urban youth are advantaged with respect to rural youth in terms of education attainment;

■ Male and female youth in rural areas find employment more quickly than their counterparts in urban areas, suggesting that finding work is particularly problematic in urban areas; and

■ Those who never enrolled in school start work at the age of 14.4 years on average, which is lower than their educated counterparts. This is more pronounced for rural female youth who never enrolled in school.

Summary of Recommendations

This chapter has shown that there is a positive correlation between training and wages. In other words, the more training a worker follows, the higher his or her wages. The government should encourage foreign companies already operating in the country with the expertise to train local workers to do so, or send them to local training institutions.

Although high quality training is important, this alone is not sufficient. The government should also pursue economic policies that stimulate business creation and growth, which will lead to job creation.

Areas for Further Study

Based on the data above, the following key questions warrant further research:

- Are those who stay at school getting the necessary skills to be attractive to the job market?
- Does the current training system provide the skills that employers are looking for?
- Why are so many educated youth not employed?
- Why are the rates of unemployment and joblessness lowest for 15 to 17 year olds?
- What does it take to obtain good quality jobs?

Notes

1. Data used so far in this survey (namely, the 2008 Gambia Joint Rural Labor Force/CDDP Baseline Survey) do not permit an analysis of the composition of youth employment. For this reason, the analysis carried out in this section is based on the 2002/03 Gambia Integrated Household Survey on Consumption Expenditure and Poverty Level Assessment. However it is worth mentioning the major caveat concerning this source, related to the definition of employment and unemployment. The questionnaire used in the IHS does not allow us to construct the ILO criteria-based indicators of employment and unemployment. For the purpose of the analysis in this section, our procedure was to define employment and unemployment in terms of respondents' responses about their employment status.

2. Lack of information on the age at which a person left school makes it impossible to distinguish between the effect of human capital on the employment probability per se, and that resulting from experience. (Guarcello et al., 2006).

3. Etude Economique Conseil, Investment Climate Survey, Employee questionnaire.

4. The reservation wage is the lowest wage at which somebody would accept a job.

CHAPTER 3

Children's Work and Schooling

Introduction

This chapter examines children's education in order to obtain an accurate picture of how youth employment outcomes are affected by low levels of human capital. While youth aged 15 to 19 years are defined as teenagers and those aged 20 to 24 years as young adults, children are youths aged seven to 14 years. More specifically, this chapter looks at children's patterns of time use, focusing in particular on the extent of child work and education. When the rewards of education are perceived to be low by parents, investment in children's education may be negatively affected. Poor employment prospects, low expected returns on human capital investments and difficult labor market transitions may serve as disincentives for parents to invest in their children's schooling. Instead, they may be lead to prematurely send their children to work, creating a cycle of poverty. Child labor is associated with compromised education, which in turn makes young people more vulnerable to low paid, insecure work and joblessness.

Involvement in Employment

The analyses on employment are based on data from the 2008 Gambia Joint Rural Labor Force/Community-Driven Development Project (CDDP Baseline Survey), a survey designed to study the participation in and characteristics of the Gambian rural labor force. The survey contained a specific section on children's time uses, including children's employment and household chores, and working hours. It should be pointed out however, that this survey unfortunately did not collect information on the status and sector of employment, meaning that it is not possible to describe the nature of children's work with this survey. For this reason, the analysis of the nature of children's work is based on the 2002/03 Gambia Integrated Household Survey on Consumption Expenditure and Poverty Level Assessment.[1]

Child work is not uncommon in The Gambia. An estimated 36 percent, or over 80,000 children in absolute terms, were in employment (see Box 3.1 on terminology, and Appendix C) in the 2008 reference year (2008 RY).[2] The child population is divided into four distinct activity groups: (i) children only in employment, (ii) children only attending school, (iii) children combining school and employment, and (iv) inactive children, doing neither. This disaggregation indicates that 27 percent of all children work and attend school at the same time, whereas nine percent are in employment and do not go to school. A further 52 percent of all children only attend school, whereas the remaining 12 percent is inactive. The data shows that, at this stage in life, almost 50 percent of all chil-

Box 3.1: Children's Work and Child Labor: A Note on Terminology

Terminology and concepts used for categorizing children's work and child labor (and in distinguishing between the two) are inconsistent in published statistics and research reports, frequently creating confusion and complicating cross-country and longitudinal comparisons. In this study, the following terminology is used

Children's Work	All productive activities performed by children.
Productive Activities	All activities whose performance can be delegated to another person with the same desired results. This includes production of all goods and the provision of services within or outside the individual's household.
Children in Employment	All market production and certain types of nonmarket production activities, including production of goods for own use.
Children in other Productive Activities	Productive activities falling outside the SNA production definition. Mainly work activities performed by household members in service to the household and its members.

Figure 3.1: Distribution of Children's Time Use by Category of Activity, 2008 RY (percent)

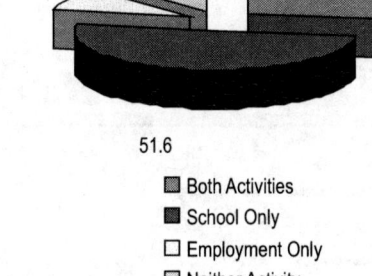

- Both Activities
- School Only
- Employment Only
- Neither Activity

Source: UCW calculations based on Joint Rural Labor Force/CDDP Baseline Survey, 2008.

dren are at risk of never receiving any formal education or of compromising their education because they have to combine work and school, are employed, or are inactive (see Figure 3.1).

Gender

Boys in the 7 to 14 years age group are somewhat more likely to be in employment than girls of the same age. Boys' employment in this age group is 38 percent, against 35 percent for girls (see Table 3.1).

Table 3.2 presents a breakdown of child activity (covers children aged 5 to 14 years) for a subsample of ECOWAS countries. Compared with other countries, the percentage of child employment in The Gambia is comparatively low.

Table 3.1: Children's Activity Status, by Gender, 2008 RY

	Male		Female		Total	
	Number	%	Number	%	Number	%
Employment Only	11,277	9.9	10,019	8.6	21,296	9.2
School Only	58,246	51.0	60,709	52.3	118,955	51.6
Both Activities	31,739	27.8	30,201	26.0	61,940	26.9
Neither Activity	12,935	11.3	15,241	13.1	28,176	12.2
Total Employment [a]	43,016	37.7	40,221	34.6	83,237	36.1
Total School [b]	89,985	78.8	90,910	78.3	180,895	78.5

Source: UCW calculations based on Joint Rural Labour Force/CDDP Baseline Survey, 2008.
Note: (a) Refers to all children in employment, regardless of school status; (b) Refers to all children attending school, regardless of work status.

Table 3.2: Child Activity in ECOWAS, 5-14 Years Age Group (percent)

	Work Only	School Only	Both	Neither	Year
Benin	26.3	18.7	39.5	15.5	2006
Burkina Faso	26.7	25.5	11.2	36.6	2006
Côte d'Ivoire	20.2	34.0	19.6	26.2	2006
The Gambia	12.6	41.9	23.8	21.7	2005
Ghana	8.5	48.2	35.0	8.4	2006
Guinea-Bissau	20.4	30.0	26.9	22.7	2006
Liberia	16.4	23.8	16.3	43.5	2007
Niger	28.8	17.7	12.6	40.8	2006
Senegal	9.9	44.6	5.6	39.8	2005
Sierra Leone	20.3	29.5	38.2	12.0	2005
Togo	10.6	50.2	22.3	16.9	2006
Average	**18.2**	**33.1**	**22.8**	**25.8**	

Source: Understanding Children's Work (UCW) country statistics.

However, those of The Gambia and other ECOWAS countries are much higher than other Latin American and Asian countries (see Figure 3.2). The percentage of economically active children in Asia and the Pacific, Latin America and the Caribbean, and the world are 18.8 percent, 5.1 percent, and 15.8 percent respectively. That of Sub-Saharan Africa is 26.4 percent (ILO, 2006).

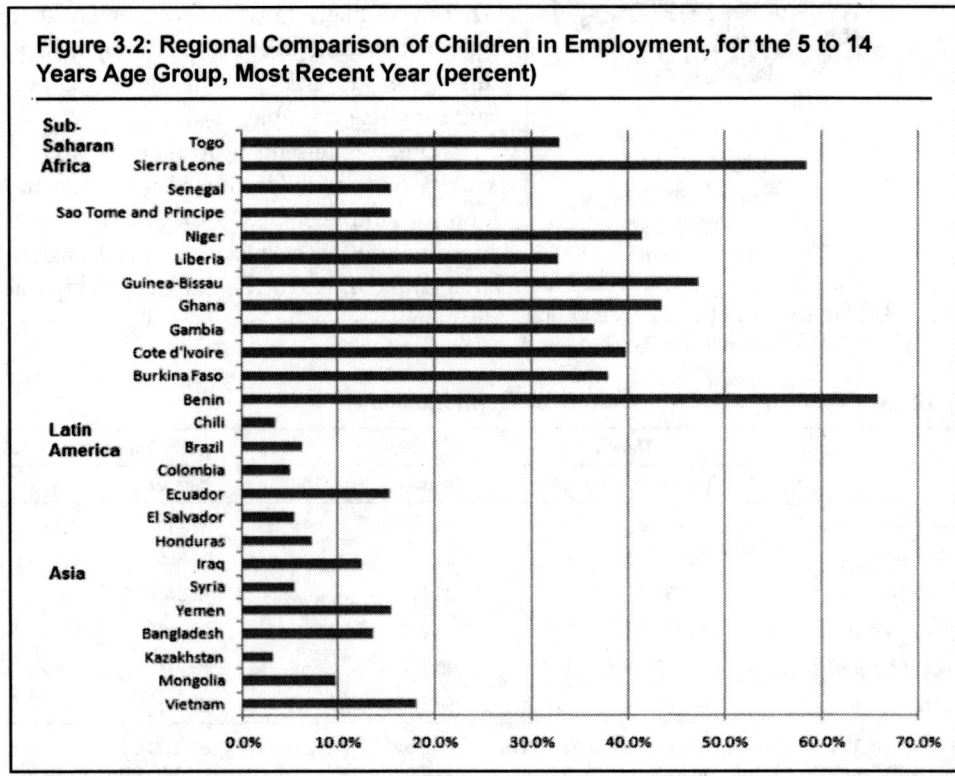

Figure 3.2: Regional Comparison of Children in Employment, for the 5 to 14 Years Age Group, Most Recent Year (percent)

Source: Understanding Children's Work (UCW).

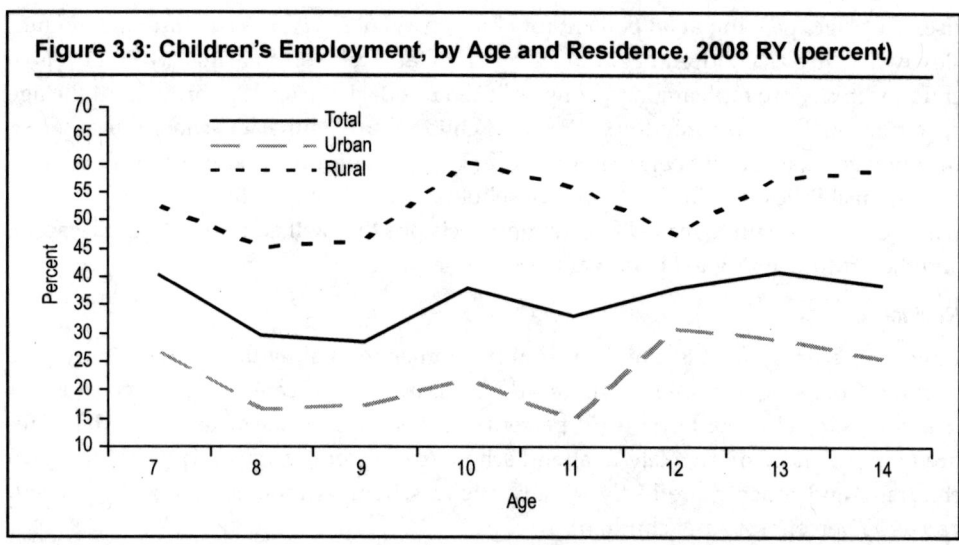

Figure 3.3: Children's Employment, by Age and Residence, 2008 RY (percent)

Source: UCW calculations based on Joint Rural Labour Force/CDDP Baseline Survey, 2008.

Age

Child employment rises with age, but the percentage of very young children who are working is far from negligible (see Figure 3.3). Approximately 29 percent of children aged nine years and 38 percent of those aged 12 years are already in employment. These very young child workers constitute a particular policy concern as they are most vulnerable to workplace abuses, and most at risk of work related ill health or injury. They are also most likely to see their education compromised.

Figure 3.4 illustrates children's transitions from inactivity to school and work. Many children start working at an early age, with adverse consequences for their development: about 30 percent of children are in employment by the age of 8 years. Employment reaches 39 percent at 11 years and 41 percent at 13 years. School attendance also

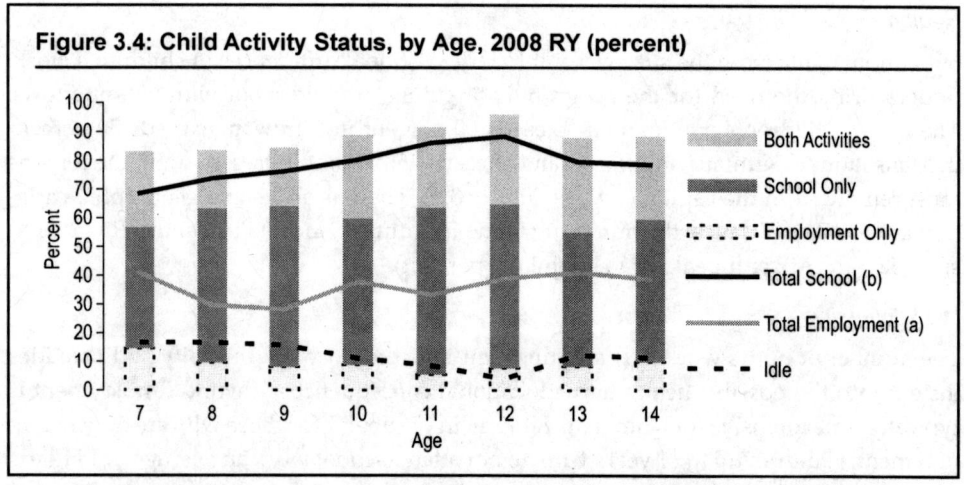

Figure 3.4: Child Activity Status, by Age, 2008 RY (percent)

Source: UCW calculations based on Joint Rural Labour Force/CDDP Baseline Survey, 2008.
Note: (a) Refers to all children in employment, regardless of school status; (b) Refers to all children attending school, regardless of employment status.

rises with age, peaking at 88 percent for children aged 12 years. Thereafter, attendance slowly declines as children begin to leave school and take on full-time work. Levels of child inactivity are high among young children but decline steadily throughout the age spectrum. At 12 years, only four percent of children are neither in school nor at work. Beyond age 12, inactivity begins to rise again, as more children assume full-time domestic responsibilities within their own households. This illustrates the very young age at which children begin to make life-changing decisions that will affect their human capital and their future ability to obtain paid employment.

Residence

Children's employment is mainly a rural phenomenon, mainly due to agriculture. The likelihood of being in employment for urban children (23 percent) is considerably lower than for their rural counterparts (53 percent), at every age. At the same time, urban children are generally more likely to attend school (84 percent, versus 71 percent for rural children), and much more likely to only attend school, without working (66 percent, versus 33 percent for rural children).

Table 3.3: Children's Activity Status, by Residence, 2008 RY

	Urban		Rural		Total	
	Number	%	Number	%	Number	%
Employment Only	6,259	4.8	15,037	14.9	21,296	9.2
School Only	85,429	66.0	33,526	33.2	118,955	51.6
Both Activities	23,617	18.2	38,323	38.0	61,940	26.9
Neither Activity	14,141	10.9	14,035	13.9	28,176	12.2
Total Employment [a]	29,876	23.0	53,360	52.9	83,237	36.1
Total School [b]	109,046	84.2	71,849	71.2	180,895	78.5

Source: UCW calculations based on Joint Rural Labour Force/CDDP Baseline Survey, 2008.
Note: (a) Refers to all children in employment, regardless of school status; (b) Refers to all children attending school, regardless of work status.

Region

Subnational data from the survey point to large regional differences in children's work, underscoring the need for the geographic targeting of child labor elimination efforts. The rate of children's employment exceeds 60 percent in Kerewan, exceeds 50 percent in Mansakonko, Kuntaur and Basse, and exceeds 45 percent in Janjanbureh, the regions most remote from the capital city (see Figure 3.5). There is also some geographic variation in school attendance, the minimum being in Kuntaur, located in Central River Division (52 percent), and peaking in Banjul (90 percent).

Work Intensity

The number of hours worked is an important indicator of work intensity and provides insight into the possible health and educational consequences of work. Employment is typically time intensive for Gambian children, in particular for those who are only in employment. Children up to 11 years who do not attend school work an average of 18 hours each week. Children of the same age group that combine employment and schooling log only slightly fewer hours (14 hours per week), underscoring the additional constraint

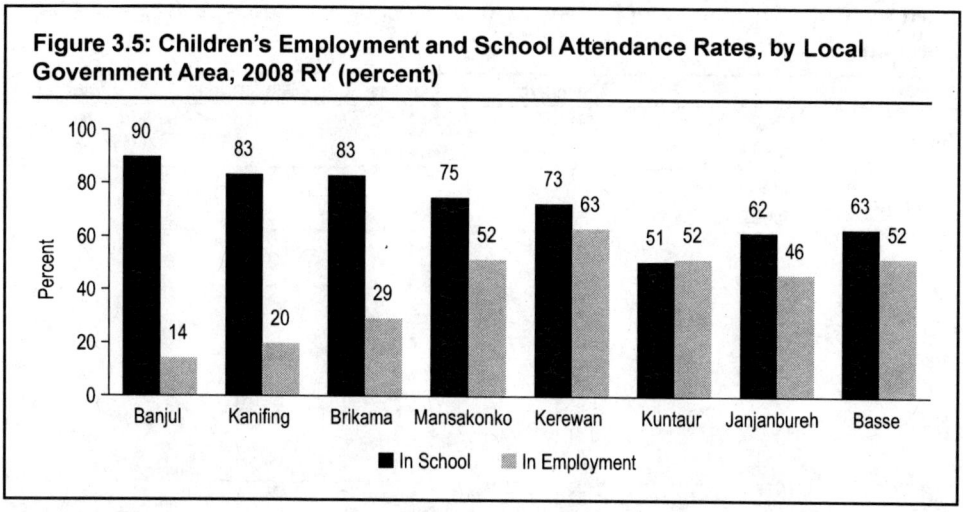

Figure 3.5: Children's Employment and School Attendance Rates, by Local Government Area, 2008 RY (percent)

Source: UCW calculations based on Joint Rural Labour Force/CDDP Baseline Survey, 2008.

that work places on children's study time, and their probable educational outcomes. Work intensity increases with age to 26 hours per week for children aged 12 to 14 years who do not attend school. It is worth noting that the number of hours worked does not vary much by gender (see Table 3.4).

Table 3.4: Children's Average Workload, by Work Status, Age Group, Gender and Residence, 2008 RY (hours per week)

	7-11 Years			12-14 Years		
	Work Only	Work and Study	Total	Work Only	Work and Study	Total
Total	17.6	13.9	14.9	26.1	12.7	16.1
Male	19.0	13.2	14.7	25.7	13.5	16.8
Female	16.0	14.6	15.2	26.4	12.0	15.5
Urban	14.5	8.0	9.5	25.1	11.3	15.2
Rural	18.2	15.4	16.3	26.5	13.3	16.5

Source: UCW calculations based on Joint Rural Labour Force/CDDP Baseline Survey, 2008.

Types of Work Performed by Children

The industrial sector in which children in employment work, and the specific modalities under which they work also vary (see Table 3.5). Children work overwhelmingly in the agriculture sector. Indeed, almost 92 percent of children in employment work in agriculture, against seven percent in services and less than one percent in manufacturing. There is surprisingly little variation by age or gender in the economic activities performed by children. There are larger differences in the nature of children's employment by place of residence. While agricultural work predominates in rural areas (94 percent), service sector work is more important in urban areas (46 percent).

Table 3.5: Children's Sector of Employment, by Gender, Residence, and Age, 2003 RY (percent)

		Agriculture	Services	Manufacturing	Total
Gender	Male	94.9	4.4	0.7	100
	Female	90.1	9.4	0.6	100
Residence	Urban	54.5	45.5	0.0	100
	Rural	93.9	5.5	0.6	100
Age	7	94.5	3.3	2.2	100
	8	95.6	4.4	0.0	100
	9	93.3	6.7	0.0	100
	10	92.0	8.0	0.0	100
	11	92.1	7.9	0.0	100
	12	91.8	8.2	0.0	100
	13	94.1	5.9	0.0	100
	14	86.3	11.5	2.2	100
Total		**92.4**	**7.0**	**0.6**	**100**

Source: UCW calculations based on Gambia Integrated Household Survey on Consumption Expenditure and Poverty Level Assessment, 2002/03.

The majority of children in employment work for their families as unpaid labor on the family farm, with little variation by age, place of residence or gender. Very few economically active children (less than one percent) work as paid employees in the formal sector. However, the data suggests that in the urban areas 33 percent of children work as paid employees and almost 46 percent work in the service sector, which is most likely retail trade work in the informal sector. This is important not only because children in the informal sector are not typically accessible to labor inspection regimes, but also because children in the services sector work outside the confines of the family, therefore putting them at higher risk of ill-treatment.

Table 3.6: Children's Modality of Employment, by Age, Gender and Residence, 2003 RY (percent)

		Paid Employee	Self-employed	Family Helper	Total
Age	7	0.0	19.7	80.3	100
	8	0.0	3.2	96.8	100
	9	0.0	17.8	82.2	100
	10	3.9	7.0	89.2	100
	11	0.0	17.5	82.5	100
	12	8.0	19.7	72.3	100
	13	2.3	18.2	79.5	100
	14	5.2	11.3	83.5	100
Gender	Male	3.8	16.4	79.8	100
	Female	1.8	12.0	86.2	100
Residence	Urban	32.7	20.6	46.7	100
	Rural	1.5	13.9	84.6	100
Total		2.8	14.2	83.0	100

Source: UCW calculations based on Gambia Integrated Household Survey on Consumption Expenditure and Poverty Level Assessment, 2002/03.

Conclusions on Children's Time Use

From the analyses detailed above, the following main points emerge about children's time use:

- Children begin work at an early age, as early as eight years, especially in rural areas;
- Children in urban areas are much more likely to attend school and not work at the same time. In rural areas, children are more likely to combine school and work, working on average 14 hours a week;
- Whereas almost all children in rural areas work as helpers on the family farm, nearly 46 percent of children in urban areas work in the service sector; and
- The data on the transition from inactivity to school and work emphasizes the fact that, at about 12 years of age, children begin to leave school to begin full-time work.

Determinants of Children's Time Use

The 2008 Gambia Joint Rural Labor Force/CDDP Baseline Survey contains individual data (such as age, gender, employment status, schooling, etc.) and some limited household data (such as family spending, access to piped water, residence area, etc.). In order to identify the factors influencing household decisions regarding children's involvement in work, and capture the effects of a set of relevant variables, we have run estimations with a bivariate probit model.[3]

Gender

When household income, parents' education, and other relevant factors are constant, there is an apparent gender bias in the allocation of children's time. Boys are three percent more likely to be in employment only and seven percent less likely to only attend school than girls. It is worth noting that the definition of employment does not include household chores that are typically carried out by girls. At the same time, girls are two percent more likely to be idle and six percent less likely to combine work with school than boys.

Household Composition

The presence of an additional child under four years in the household reduces the probability of children combining school and work by three percent and increases the probability of idleness by two percent. This might be because older children have to take care of their younger siblings. In fact, the presence of babies in the family raises the probability of older siblings being in employment without attending school by one percent.

Household Income and Access to Piped Water[4]

Econometric evidence confirms the importance of household income (household spending is used as a proxy) in the decisions concerning children's time use (see Appendix B). Twice the amount of household spending is associated with a two percent reduction in both the probability of employment only and the probability of idleness, and with over a two percent increase in the probability of combining work with school. It does not have a significant effect on the probability of only attending school. Interestingly, this suggests that children who are in employment will still work even if household income doubles, which means that children will most likely be combining some degree of work with education. In the future it will be important to conduct further analysis on work intensity in order to ascertain the degree to which having to work affects children's education.

Consistent with findings from other countries and samples, access to piped water is a relevant predictor of children's time use, being associated with a six percent higher probability of being in school and a four percent lower probability both of working, and of being idle. This large effect might be because of the genuine impact of water access, as water fetching is often a time consuming activity delegated to children, but it might also capture some other effects, as this variable could proxy for households' socio-economic status, or the level of development in the area of residence.

Gender and Education of the Head of Household

There are significant differences in the likelihood of children attending school and working, according to the gender of the head of household. Compared to children in female headed households, children in households headed by a male are six percent more likely to be in employment, 10 percent less likely to attend school, and four percent more likely to be idle. This is surprising, as it is usually assumed that female headed households are poorer and therefore less likely to send their children to school.[5]

The effect of an increase in the parents' education levels on children's time use is remarkably strong. When income and other factors are constant, children from households whose head has at least primary education are six percent less likely to only work, relative to children from households whose head is uneducated. If the household head has secondary or higher education[6] the likelihood of children working without attending school falls by a further two percent. Parental education is associated with a higher probability of school attendance and a lower probability of idleness. The probability of attending school increases by eight percent if the household head has primary education and by 17 percent if the household head has higher education. Children in households whose head has secondary or higher education are seven percent less likely to be idle than those in a household headed by an uneducated adult.

Place of Residence

The likelihood of attending school and being in employment varies significantly by place of residence. When other factors are constant, children living in urban areas are 14 percent more likely to just study, six percent less likely to just work, and eight percent less likely to combine school and work, compared with their rural counterparts. There are pronounced differences in children's time use across local government areas. Children from Basse, located in the most remote region, and the reference category, display the highest probability of only working (12 percent higher than children from Banjul) and the lowest probability of attending school without working (36 percent lower than children from Banjul).

Given the significant difference between labor markets in urban and rural areas, estimations were also carried out separately for each (see Appendix Tables B.2 and B.3). The main differences between the urban and rural estimations are discussed below. Gender bias in children's time use is greater in rural areas. Boys in rural areas are six percent more likely both to only work and to combine work with school, and eight percent less likely to only attend school, compared with girls in rural areas. This is surprising given that in most Sub-Saharan African countries girls living in rural areas are less likely to attend school. At the same time, gender differences in children's employment and school attendance in urban areas are not significant.

In relation to the individual and household information mentioned above, the following points were noted after disaggregating the data by geographic location:

- The impact of household spending on how children spend their time is greater in urban areas than in rural areas;
- Access to piped water decreases the probability of only being in employment in both urban and rural areas. At the same time, access to piped water is associated with a seven percent higher probability of only studying in urban areas, whereas in rural areas the impact on the probability of only attending school is not significant;
- Children are more likely to only work and less likely to only attend school in male headed households, in both urban and rural areas;
- The level of education of the household head has more pronounced impacts in rural areas on both the probability of being in employment only, and of only studying than in urban areas; and
- Children's time use differs substantially by local government area in both urban and rural settings. Children from both rural and urban parts of the Basse area display the highest probability of only working and the lowest probability of only attending school.

As evidenced above, the main determinants of children's time use are gender, the education level of the head of household, and the place of residence. However, children's employment is a complex phenomenon and the factors mentioned above only partially explain the determinants of children's time allocation. Better data and more in-depth analysis are needed for a fuller understanding of why children work. Information on the availability of infrastructure, school quality, and access to credit markets and social protection schemes is especially needed. Better qualitative analyses of factors such as parental attitudes and cultural norms would also be useful.

Summary of Recommendations

There are three types of measures to tackle child labor issues:

- For children at risk of being involved in child labor, *preventive measures* are necessary. It is however necessary to first conduct more in-depth research and address the specific factors causing children to work. Working is rarely children's choice but often it is part of family plans to reduce household vulnerability. Reducing household vulnerability without child labor would be possible by expanding social protection schemes such as conditional cash transfer programs, social pension programs, and child and disability grants.
- For children already working, *second chance* measures should be implemented, enabling them to enjoy formal education and the subsequent prospects. This might be achieved by providing special remedial support and "catch-up" education with separate and intensive courses.

   ▨   Finally, *direct action* measures are necessary to identify the most vulnerable children who are facing immediate and severe threats to survival, and withdraw them from the workplace.

In order to make any of these three measures a reality, a favorable enabling environment is required, including political commitment, an appropriate legal framework, capable institutions, and a mobilized society.

Areas for Further Study

Based on the data above, the following key questions warrant further research:

   ▨   Why are there so many school dropouts and early school leavers?

   ▨   Approximately 29 percent of children aged nine years and 38 percent of children aged 12 years are already in employment. How should policy-makers address this concern?

   ▨   The rate of children's employment exceeds 45 percent (or in some cases 60 percent) in the most remote regions. School attendance varies between 52 percent and 90 percent. How can one explain these regional differences?

   ▨   Children aged 7 to 11 years in employment and who do not attend school work an average of 18 hours per week. Children of the same age group that combine employment and schooling log only slightly fewer hours. How can the education system be adjusted to meet the needs of these children and provide them with an opportunity to succeed?

Notes

1. However, it is worth mentioning again the major caveat concerning this source, related to the definition of employment and unemployment. The questionnaire used in the IHS does not allow us to construct the ILO criteria-based indicators of employment and unemployment. For the purpose of the analysis in this section, our procedure was to define employment and unemployment in terms of respondents' responses about their employment status.

2. In accordance with the standards for national child labor statistics set at the 18th International Conference of Labour Statisticians (Res. II), the study distinguishes between two broad categories of child workers: children in employment and children in other productive activities. The definition of children in employment in turn derives from the System of National Accounts (SNA) (Rev. 1993), the conceptual framework that sets the international statistical standards for the measurement of the market economy.

3. The bivariate probit model was used to jointly determine the correlated decisions on child schooling and work. A simple economic model of household behavior is used to guide the empirical specification. For detailed information on the model, see Cigno et al., 2002. The analysis is obviously conditioned by the information available. Notwithstanding the extensiveness of the survey utilized, potentially important variables are missing. In particular, information on the relative price of child work is difficult to capture: indicators of the returns on education and work are not easily available. For a discussion of the role played by unobservable factors, see Deb and Rosati, 2002.

4. Access to piped water is defined as access to drinking water either from an indoors/compound tap, or from a public standard pipe.

5. However, the 2009 Poverty Assessment found that there are more male headed households living in poverty. The assessment postulated that this might be because many female headed households received remittances from spouses abroad.

6. The higher education category includes post-secondary vocational schools, colleges, post O-Level vocational and technical schools, universities, and master and PhD. programs.

CHAPTER 4

Provision of Technical and Vocational Education and Training

Introduction

The persistence of poverty in the face of sustained economic growth has brought about the need to rethink development strategies in order to reorient the country toward employment intensive economic growth. As a result, the government formulated the National Employment Policy and Action Plan as a way of redistributing the benefits of growth, reducing poverty, and raising living standards.

In this respect, the Ministry of Trade, Industry and Employment put in place appropriate policy strategies and institutional mechanisms for the implementation of the employment policy action plan as part of the Poverty Reduction Strategic Paper (PRSP). These aim to ensure that national goals and objectives on reducing unemployment, underemployment, and poverty are achieved, specifically in relation to youth and women. The Gambia Jobs Project, a project developed to implement the action plan's priority programs, has received funds from the government and UNDP. The project has the potential to create 10,000 jobs per year, for five years.

As the government steps up efforts to generate employment, there is also the need to ensure that citizens, especially the unskilled youth, obtain the skills necessary to benefit from the jobs that are or will in the future become available. As the national employment plan states: "In the last decade the government is increasingly seeing vocational training and skills development as integral parts of broad economic strategies to further develop the economy and promote employment opportunities."

This chapter provides an overview of the current Technical and Vocational Education and Training (TVET) sector. It will address the question of how ongoing TVET reforms relate to skill demand in the growing and emerging sectors of the economy, and provide recommendations on how to improve the system for youth training and employment, keeping in mind the key findings from the previous chapters on children's' and youth's time use.

Provision of Technical and Vocational Education and Training

TVET provision consists of several dimensions (see Figure 4.1), including pre employment training provided by government institutions, NGOs and private training bodies. In addition, enterprise based training is a major source of skills acquisition for those in employment, be it paid employment or in the informal sector. The vast majority of skills training is provided by the private sector.

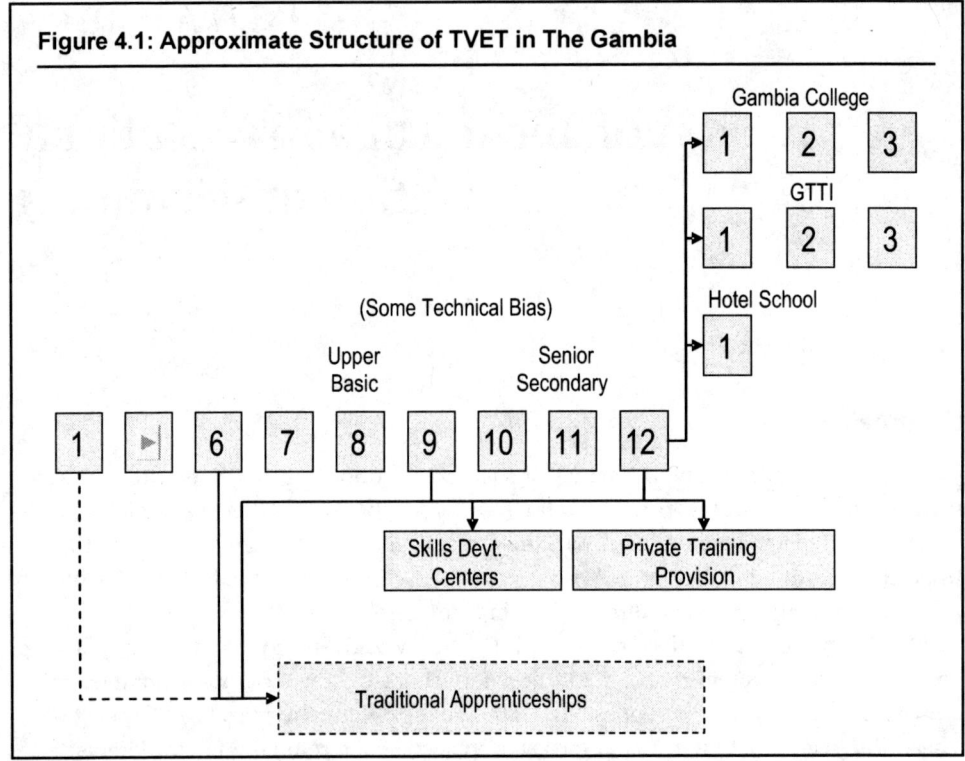

Figure 4.1: Approximate Structure of TVET in The Gambia

Note: Excludes the Management Development Institute and the Gambia Telecommunications and Multimedia Institute.

The main training providers are the following, in order of prevalence: private training providers, including community based organizations and nongovernmental organizations (CBOs/NGOs), and public training institutions. In addition, enterprise based training, or "traditional apprenticeship," is a major source of skills acquisition for those in employment, especially for young men in the informal sector. Public training institutions tend to be concentrated in Banjul and at the postsecondary level. The premier institution is The Gambia Technical Training Institute which provides certificate and diploma courses at the postsecondary level (grade 12 entry).

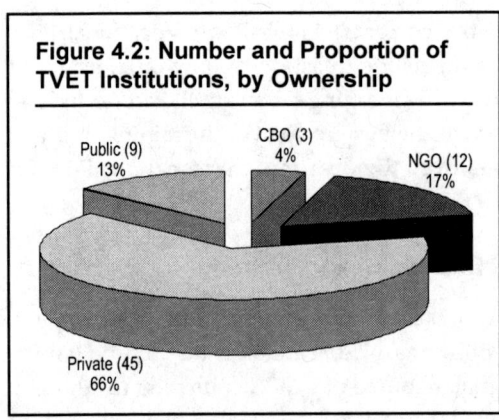

Figure 4.2: Number and Proportion of TVET Institutions, by Ownership

Source: Labor Market Information Department—National Training Authority.

Sixty six percent of the current 69 training providers are privately owned, 17 percent are run by NGOs, four percent by CBOs and only 13 percent by the government (see Figure 4.2). Total enrollment and annual output for 2006 are given in Table 4.1.

About 7,900 trainees were enrolled in 2006, providing a total of 5,000 graduates. Of these, Information and Communication Technology (ICT) courses

Table 4.1: TVET Enrollment (in Descending Order) and Graduates, by Subject, 2006

	Enrollment			Graduates	
	Total (Number)	Total (%)	Female (%)	Total (Number)	% of Enrollment
ICT	2,779	35.2	44.3	2,110	75.9
Management	1,102	14.1	47.4	754	68.4
Bookkeeping & Accounting	1,048	13.3	52.3	765	73.0
Secretarial	784	9.9	84.3	197	25.1
Tailoring & Cooking	760	9.6	55.8	230	30.3
Languages	694	8.8	42.8	493	71.0
Travel & Tourism	272	3.4	31.6	253	93.0
Electrical & Electronics	200	2.5	12.0	79	39.5
Horticulture	52	0.7	78.8	42	80.8
Banking & Finance	50	0.6	34.0	11	22.0
Construction	42	0.5	4.8	20	47.6
Welding & Fabrication	29	0.4	3.5	8	27.6
Motor Mechanics	16	0.2	12.5	9	56.3
Other	60	0.8	30.0	30	50.0
Total	7,888	100	49.1	5,001	63.4

Source: Labor Market Information System—National Training Authority.

attracted most of the trainees (35.2 percent; and 42.2 percent of the graduates), followed by business subjects (38 percent).[1] Thus, ICT and business courses trained over 70 percent of all students. Female trainees accounted for almost half the enrollments, and were strongly represented in bookkeeping and accounting, secretarial skills, home science (sewing, tailoring, and cooking) and horticulture. Enrollments in traditional vocational courses appear to be understated in the database. For example, it is unlikely that only 16 people were enrolled in motor mechanics throughout the country. Enrollment in agriculture and horticulture also seems particularly low given the dependence on this sector for employment, and its share of GDP. The output to enrollment ratio probably reflects courses' length more than completion rates. However, the low ratios for secretarial skills, tailoring and cooking, banking and finance, and welding and fabrication may warrant further investigation.

Public Training Provision

Training provision by the public sector is relatively limited. It is provided by nine government-owned training centers, that are:

- The GTTI, which is autonomous;
- The Hotel School;
- The Gambia College (for agriculture);
- The Rural Skills Training Center at Mansa Konko;
- The Julangel Skills Training Center;
- The Kotu (NAWEC) In-house Training Center;
- The President's Award Scheme Skills Training Center;

■ The Gambia Telecommunication and Multimedia Institute (GTMI); and
■ The Management Development Institute (MDI).

The GTTI. Due to its size and role, the GTTI is worthy of particular mention. It was established in Banjul by an Act of Parliament in 1983. Its mandate is to train middle-level manpower in commerce, business, accounting, engineering, and construction. The GTTI is an autonomous body reporting to the Ministry of Higher Education, Research, Science and Technology. It is governed by a board of governors that consists of 12 members.[2] A private sector representative is the Deputy Chair of the board. GTTI employees are hired on the civil service pay scale, and receive a thirty percent premium. Appendix D shows the organizational structure of the GTTI.

The GTTI enrolled 1,401 students in its main programs in the 2005/06 academic year, plus 266 in the professional development unit in charge of in-service training, reaching a total of 1,667 trainees at its main campus. Thirty eight percent of the students are female, almost all of whom are enrolled in business studies and ICT. The statistics show a minimal attrition rate. Overall, the pass rate was 87 percent. Enrollment appears to be growing rapidly, particularly in the engineering department, where it increased from 339 students in 2005/06 to 611 students in 2007/08. Overall enrollment was 1,655 students in 2008, plus 136 in the professional development unit and 348 at the Banjul Skills Training Center.

Table 4.2: GTTI Enrollment, Graduates and Pass Rate, by Department and Gender, 2005/06

	Enrollment (Number)			Graduates (Number)			Pass Rate (%)
	Male	Female	Total	Male	Female	Total	
Construction	347	18	365	338	18	356	100
ICT	88	159	247	88	159	247	93
Engineering	322	17	339	316	15	331	86
Business Studies	215	335	550	188	271	459	73
Subtotal	972	529	1,501	930	463	1,393	87
Professional Development Unit	—	—	266	—	—	263	n.a.
Banjul Skills Training Center	387	52	439	360	48	408	78
Total	1,359*	581*	2,206	1,290*	511*	2,064	74

Source: GTTI Annual Report, 2006.
Note: * Gender totals are understated due to the unavailability of disaggregated data for the Professional Development Unit.

For the 2005/06 academic year, the institute's operating expenditures were D 16.1 million,[3] or nearly US$600,000. Government allocations represented only D 5.1 million of this (32 percent). This represented a marked change: four out of five GTTI programs were tuition free until September 1998, when cost sharing was introduced.[4] The vast majority of the institute's income is obtained from student tuition and fees, in addition to contracts and consultancies undertaken by some departments.[5] The GTTI's total operating expenditure by student (including both full-time and part-time) is D 7,666, or US$380. This is low by international standards.

According to the 2006 Annual Report, "the Institute's strategic direction continues to focus on developing its capacity to deliver quality training programs up to higher levels and organizing customized courses for both the public and private sectors of the economy. Our main focus would now be to expedite the transformation process to a higher level institution. The emergence of a new curriculum that will radically transform the Institute's opportunities to offer higher level training programs to a wider clientele is what is required in order to complement new technologies."

However, the GTTI seems to be relatively isolated from the market. Only one in 12 board members is from the private sector. It reportedly has no industrial advisory committees to help steer curriculum content. It is not clear how the GTTI gets quantitative and qualitative information about employer requirements. On the positive side, the year of industry placement that candidates undergo between the first and third years in the Engineering Department enhances the relevance of training. Entrepreneurship is probably the most important skill that can be taught given that it is key to employment growth; however, little entrepreneurship training is offered.

National Youth Service Scheme. The National Youth Service Scheme (NYSS) started in 1996 to provide youth with skills for employment. It emphasizes self-reliance and aims to discourage the rural-urban drift. It enrolls about 200 youth aged 17 to 30 years annually, based on quotas for each of the six regions. Youth are first provided with orientation to build their self-esteem and leadership abilities. Core members are exposed to various types of occupation and choose which they would like to train for. The NYSS then places them in existing training institutions for 22 months, where they receive a living allowance. The scheme operates some of the training itself, namely in horticulture at its farm, and tailoring and fashion design at its own training centers. The NYSS monitors the performance of the trainees and makes continued support conditional on performance. If attendance drops below 85 percent, the trainees do not receive their monthly stipend. The scheme also introduced an apprenticeship program in 2002, taking in youth with low levels of prior education for 46 months. Initial funds from the Highly Indebted Poor Countries initiative enabled them to do this, and a second funding agreement should help to offer more apprenticeships.

Since 1996 the NYSS has trained about 1,550 youth in 22 occupational fields. Male enrollments are by far the majority (1,227, compared with 338 of their female counterparts, or 22 percent of the intake). The fields with the highest enrollment were electricity (241), car mechanics (204), tailoring (182), carpentry (131), and electronics (114). Some agricultural occupations were included: rice agronomy (76), livestock (96), and forestry (36). Most of the trainees went to the GTTI (685), followed by the NYSS Tailoring Center (121) and various mentors and local workshops (219). Until the graduation of those who started in 2003, 77 percent of trainees finished the program (959 of 1,242).

When the scheme had about 500 graduates in 2002, UNDP financed an impact study of the NYSS, that included a tracer study that interviewed 377 graduates. It found that 57 percent were unemployed, 32 percent were in paid employment, and 11 percent were self-employed. Of the employed graduates, only 43 percent were in occupations related to the skills they acquired. Of the 41 self-employed graduates, 22 percent were in plumbing, 22 percent in electrical installation, 12 percent in sewing and tailoring and 12 percent were in masonry. Almost all graduates found the skills training useful (96 percent). Of these, half said the quality was excellent or very good and the other half said it was good.

However, most training institutions were unable to include entrepreneurial skills as a vital component of the curricula.

The NYSS' estimated cost per student was D 10,800 (US$400), excluding administrative overheads, about half of which was for monthly stipends. The study concluded that "the high level of financial investment, compared with the low level of employment of graduates in their area of training (43 percent) indicates that the current programs are not cost effective." Among the weaknesses noted were the following: (i) the orientation offered does not provide students with an indication of the market demand for each skill area; (ii) the level of training provided seems "very inadequate;" (iii) graduates are not skilled enough to be self-employed; and (iv) trainees often do not return to their places of origin because of limited employment opportunities. Hence, the scheme has not helped to minimize the rural-urban drift. The study included the following recommendations:

- Base the training offered on surveys of the job market's skill requirements;
- Use aptitude testing to screen candidates for the various occupations;
- Develop syllabi for the courses;
- Make courses more practical and provide greater training time;
- Include industrial placements for 6 to 12 months after training;
- Include intensive training in entrepreneurship;
- Provide start-up capital for graduates; and
- Develop NYSS in-house training capacity and instructors.

Private Training Provision

Private Training is available in four main formats: training provided by NGOs and CBOs, profit oriented training institutions, enterprise based training, and traditional apprenticeships, as detailed below.

Non Governmental Organizations (Nonprofit Trainers). There are about 15 NGOs and CBOs providing skills training in The Gambia. SOS Hermann Gmeiner Production and Skills Training Center in Bakoteh is one of the more prominent. The center enrolls 60 low-income students with basic education for three year courses. Students also carry out enterprise placements for six to eight weeks during their final year. The center has three workshops: carpentry, metalwork and car mechanics. SOS has six teachers, four full-time and two part-time. It receives no financial support from the government but complements its income by fabricating products in response to orders from the public and by servicing automobiles in its Production Center. The biggest problem for the center is finding employment for its trainees on completion of their training. Some get paid jobs, but most work in local workshops or become self-employed.

The Njawara Agricultural Training Center (NATC) is also worthy of mention. It is community owned and financed through a succession of donor projects. The goal is to promote self-employment and raise incomes. The center employs six full-time teaching staff plus two part-time staff. It offers:

1. Short-term training to practicing farmers in a series of six two day sessions. For this the center selects 10 villages (out of 350 in the area) and five women per village for the part-time training, which includes "step down training" to enable them to share their knowledge with others in the village. The aim is to create community gardens to produce lucrative vegetable crops.

2. A full-time nine month course which includes three months in residence with an employer, three months on the trainee's land and a final three months in the center. Course content includes basic agro-forestry, horticulture (vegetable and fruit production), livestock management (small ruminants and poultry), food processing, and marketing. In addition, it provides gender training covering leadership, ownership rights, and the empowerment of women. Trainees prepare a business plan and are introduced to microfinance at the end of the course, receiving a loan of D 23,000 (US$855) from the institution as a settlement package. The center takes on 20 trainees aged 18 to 35 years per year for its long-term courses, of which 70 percent are women, and has trained 160 people to date. No fees are charged, and demand for the training is strong: the last program attracted 130 applicants for 20 places.

3. Nursery seedlings that it produces for the communities. Indeed it produces its own dormitory furniture from the wood harvested from its fast-growing Gmalina tree production.

Many graduates have been reportedly successful in generating good incomes from the training and support received from the center. Unfortunately, it had to delay the start of training this year because of lack of funds. The main challenge appears to be how to expand the program and train more farmers.

Private Training Institutions (For Profit Trainers). About 45 private for profit training institutions have been identified by the National Training Authority. Most of these offer certificate and diploma courses in the fields of commerce, management, accounting and finance and IT.

The Quantum Net Institute of Technology (QNIT) is one of the private training providers, that enrolls about 1,000 students per year. Student fees pay for all the institution's expenses. It offers 15 courses, including an introductory program of mathematics and English for about 150 students, basic computer courses starting with a three week course on computer literacy followed by a six week intermediate and an eight week advanced course on MS Office, in addition to courses on customer service, web design and graphics. At the advanced level, it offers degree programs in computer science and business administration, on franchise from the St. Mary's University of Halifax, Canada and the University of The Gambia. Its average enrollment is of 12 to 16 students per computing course, and 40 students per diploma course.

The QNIT has eight technical teaching staff, four academic teachers, and four assistants. The management of the institution canvasses industry needs by scanning job advertisements and talking to industry representatives. It has identified the need to teach Photoshop and has organized internal training for its teaching staff in this field. There is some student dropout for financial reasons. The main constraint for the institute at present is its rented building, but it is constructing its own classroom block on land owned by the institution. Quantum Net is in process of being licensed by the National Training Authority.

Enterprise Based Training. There is no regulated system of apprenticeship in the formal private sector. However, enterprises do provide in-house training when skills are lacking. According to the NTA Enterprise Training Needs Assessment Survey of 2007, most skills acquisition takes place partly or wholly on the job (see Appendix E). About 61 percent of surveyed enterprises provided in-service training to their workers, and about 20 percent provided more organized training through the classroom and practical work. However, only seven percent of the surveyed firms had conducted training needs assessments.[6] One reason that enterprises do not provide more training is the fear of poaching, that another firm will headhunt a trained worker, and the investment in staff training would be lost.

Traditional Apprenticeships. Traditional trade apprenticeships are probably the largest avenue for skills acquisition for young males, but the quality is uneven and low. Parents often arrange for their children, particularly boys, to be apprenticed to master craftsmen in roadside workshops. This includes traditional production such as metal-work, vehicle maintenance, carpentry, furniture making, making cooking utensils, and so on. Girls tend to be apprenticed in hairdressing, food preparation and servicing, and tailoring and sewing shops.

There is usually no formal contract for apprentices. The master craftsmen is typically not paid for training them either, but gets virtually free labor for the period of the apprenticeship. The apprentice may be paid a small allowance to cover travel, or may receive small payments when production contracts are fulfilled and paid. The training is essentially to learn by observing and participating in the production process. The length of apprenticeships varies from several months to up to 5 years. Upon completion of the apprenticeship, the apprentice is expected to seek work elsewhere. In some cases however, master craftsmen use the apprenticeship to identify and select competent workers for their own enterprises.

Financing of Education

Throughout most of the recent decade, public expenditure choices have crowded out domestic financing for education recurrent expenditure. The share of the public recurrent budget allocated to education averaged just 11 percent over the period, representing only two percent of GDP, far below the Education for All Fast Track Initiative (EFA-FTI) benchmarks, of 20 percent and 3.6 percent respectively (see Table 4.3). However, because of high debt service requirements, this share rises to an average of 18 percent of total public discretionary recurrent expenditure (excluding interest payments). Thus, within its fiscal constraints, the government commitment to the implementation of the education sector program has been high.

Table 4.3: Overview of Education Expenditure, 1997-2008

	97-98	00-01	04-05	05-06	06-07	07-08	Average 04-08	EFA-FTI Benchmark
Domestic Revenue (% of GDP)	19	17	20	21	22	22	21	14-18
Recurrent Education Expenditure (% of GDP)	2.7	2.6	1.9	2.0	2.0	2.1	2	3.6
Recurrent Education Expenditure (% of Total Recurrent Expenditure)	15	14	11	11	12	12	11	20
Recurrent Education Expenditure/ Discretionary Recurrent Expenditure	21	19	19	18	18	17	18	20
Basic Education Recurrent Expenditure (% of Recurrent Education Expenditure)		51	64	66	67	66	65	42-64

Source: Ministry of Finance, 1997-2008 budget data.

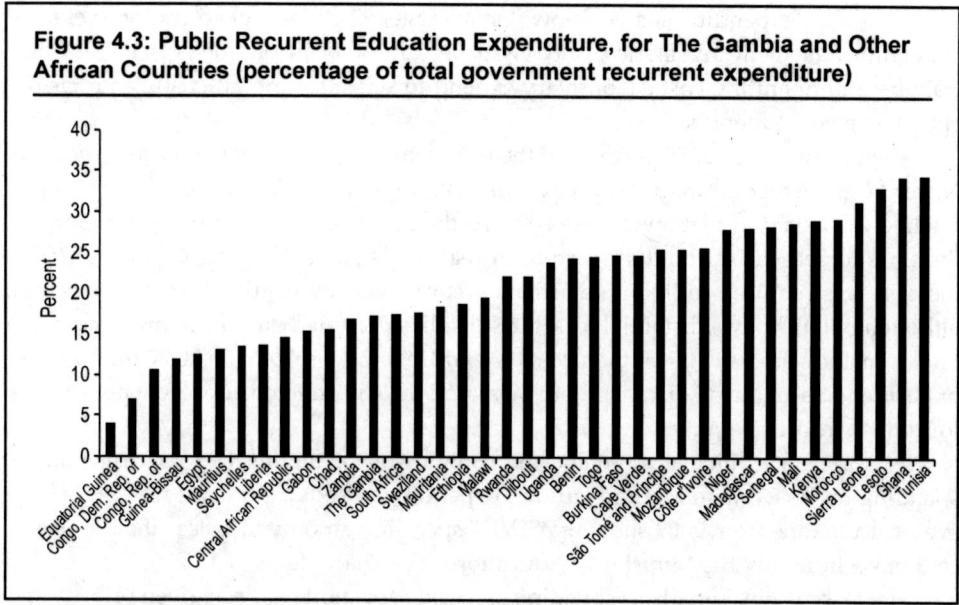

Figure 4.3: Public Recurrent Education Expenditure, for The Gambia and Other African Countries (percentage of total government recurrent expenditure)

Source: Country Rating Data, File 37, World Bank, ISU, RESEN, Pôle de Dakar, and Modèle de Simulation Année Base 2007.
Note: Latest data available: 2003-2009.

The Gambia's total public recurrent education expenditure is 17.2 percent of total government recurrent expenditure, which is four percent lower than the average of 38 African countries for which data is available (see Figure 4.3).

Figure 4.4 shows the impact of these choices on recurrent education expenditure. All categories of recurrent expenditure (salaries, goods, services and training) have either eroded or remained constant throughout most of the decade.

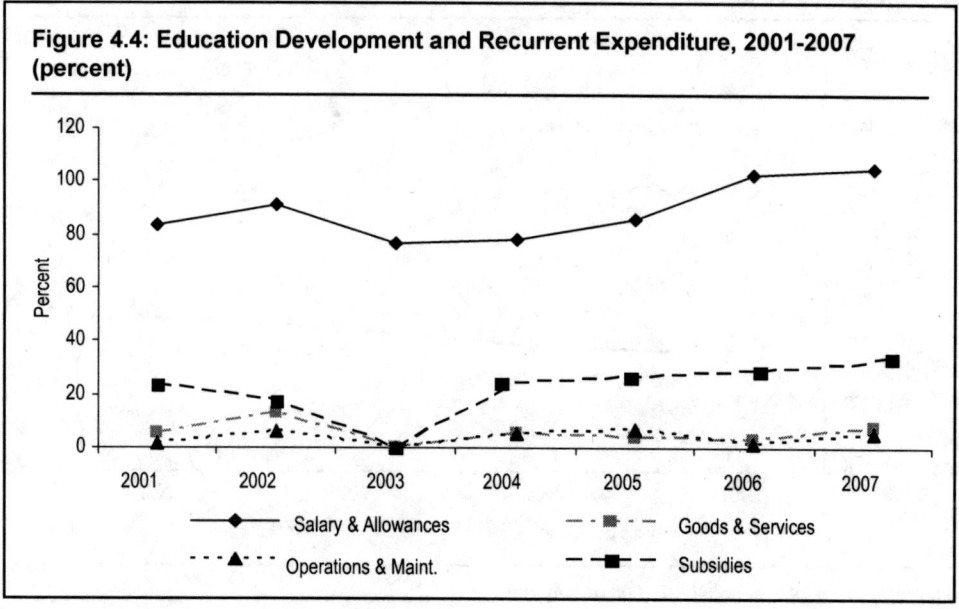

Figure 4.4: Education Development and Recurrent Expenditure, 2001-2007 (percent)

Source: Ministry of Finance, 1997-2008 budget data.

Nonsalary expenditure is very low. On average, 92 percent of education recurrent expenditure is spent on salaries; only eight percent is spent on goods, services, local training and operating costs. Nonsalary expenditure is also unpredictable and has declined on a per student basis.

A large share (about 65 percent) of the recurrent budget is spent on basic education. Nevertheless, expenditure per student is low, averaging only US$25, and has remained relatively constant at that level since 2001. At the secondary level, expenditure per student has increased by about 40 percent in real terms since 2001 (see Figure 4.5). This increase was required to liquidate arrears accumulated by nearly all schools, because although parents pay substantial fees, the subsidies provided have been historically too low to enable schools to cover their costs. To address this problem, in 2005, the Ministry of Basic and Secondary Education both increased the subsidy and adopted a per student formula to improve equity.

Data are not available to enable the comparison of the level of recurrent public spending on TVET with total government spending on education and training. However, calculations from 2002 show that TVET spending amounted to less than four percent of spending by the Ministry of Education.[7] The share devoted to TVET is likely to have decreased substantially as spending on basic education has been given priority and enrollments in basic and secondary education have increased. Government subsidies for the GTTI, on the other hand, have decreased substantially. One rough indicator of quality is the proportion of spending on nonsalary inputs. Generally for TVET, 60 percent of spending is devoted to salaries, compared with 40 percent for nonsalary inputs. In The Gambia, these proportions are biased toward salary inputs, with a share of 86.3 percent in 2006.[8]

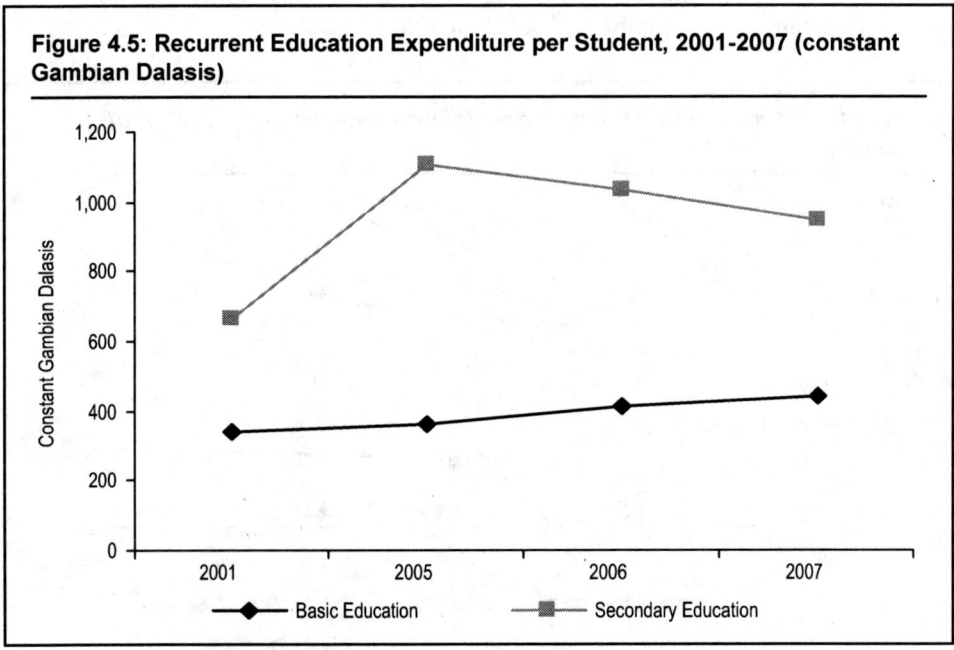

Figure 4.5: Recurrent Education Expenditure per Student, 2001-2007 (constant Gambian Dalasis)

Source: Ministry of Finance, 1997-2008 budget data.

TVET has benefited from little capital investment. Other donor financing, such as EC assistance to the NTA, has involved essentially expert services. The 2006 Public Expenditure Review includes a projection of investment requirements by level of education and training. The gap for TVET is the highest of any level of education,[9] as shown in Table 4.4.

Table 4.4: TVET Government Financing and Projected Investment Shortfall, 2006-2015

	Government Financing		Financing Gap		Total Investment Required		Overall Financing Gap (%)
	Amount	%	Amount	%	Amount	%	
Improve Access	0.00	0	3,694.41	100.0	3,694.41	1.9	100.0
Increase Relevance	—	—	2,665.96	100.0	2,665.96	1.4	100.0
Improve Quality	0.00	0	853.36	96.7	882.11	0.5	96.7
Improve Management	74.55	14.4	441.99	85.6	516.54	0.3	85.6
Predictable and Adequate Funding	—	—	55.61	100.0	55.61	0	100.0
Functional Policy and Strategic Planning Framework	—	—	26.59	100.0	26.59	0	100.0
Total	74.55	—	7,737.91	98.7	7,841.22	4.0	98.7

Source: PER 2006, Table 10.4.

It is reasonable to conclude that the bulk of the financing for skills development comes from non government sources. Only a small minority of training institutions are government owned. In addition, one distinguishing feature of TVET in The Gambia is the willingness of parents and trainees to pay for skills acquisition, even in postsecondary technical institutions. The NTA collects information on fees charged by training institutions for various courses, mainly in privately-owned institutions, through its registration process. The data show that programs in accounting, business, tourism and ICT cost D 5,000 to D 8,000 (US$186 to US$297) per six month course. A few institutions charge higher fees, in the range of D 15,000 to D 20,000 (US$558 to US$743) for one to two year programs. the GTTI charges fees at the lower end of the range: its one year programs cost about the same as six month programs in private institutions; a one year course in ICT user skills costs between D 5,200 and D 7,500 (US$193 to US$279) for a certificate or diploma; and a two year engineering course costs D 4,700 to D 8,500 (US$175 to US$315). Despite this, the GTTI is still able to raise two thirds of its revenue from student fees and service contracts.

In contrast, NTA data show that fees at vocational institutions are generally much lower than in technical institutes. The Njawara Agricultural Training Center charges no fees at all. The NGO WEC Wellingara Skill Center charges only D 600 (US$22) per year and Bokalaho Skills Training Center charges D 1,500 (US$56). One reason is that such training centers are typically community or NGO owned and operated, and seek to reach lower income groups as part of their mission.

Recent TVET Reforms

The 2002 TVET policy aims "to ensure an adequate response to labor market requirements in all sectors, having regard to globalization and regionalization, and to provide opportunities for life-long learning." The policy recommended an institutional and legislative framework for the development of TVET, centered on the establishment of a national training authority. It noted that employers and communities were "disenfranchised" from providing input and direction into TVET policy development. As laid out in the policy, the national training authority would be a semi-autonomous organization partnering the private sector with government. It would be responsible for providing advice, setting standards, regulating providers and coordinating the provision of TVET.

The policy also noted the urgent need for better labor market information on which to base the identification of skills gaps and requirements, and referred to the lack of investment in TVET and the capacity of training institutions as constraints on success, resulting from the lack of essential financing, particularly for needed expansion and improvements. To mobilize resources a financial framework featuring the establishment of a training levy based on 0.25 percent of the overall revenue of a firm was recommended. More information on the national training authority and the levy are provided below.

The 2007-2015 Poverty Reduction Strategy Paper II (PRSP II) also sets targets for TVET (see Box 4.1). To achieve these, the following interventions will be undertaken: improve access, relevance, quality and sector management; make funding predictable and adequate; and prepare a Functional Policy and Strategic Framework.

Box 4.1: The PRSP II Specific Objectives

- Increase the number of TVET institutions by 50 percent;
- Increase the number of skills' development centers in rural areas;
- Approve a system of prior learning accreditation;
- Establish a Labor Market Information System (LMIS);
- Establish mechanical and engineering laboratories;
- Approve syllabi;
- Make TVET affordable to 90 percent of all eligible trainees;
- Increase the number of students with disabilities in TVET to 50 percent;
- Achieve a 75 percent retention rate in the TVET system;
- Achieve gender parity in TVET;
- Collect at least 75 percent of the total expected fees; and
- Establish a functional National Vocational Qualification Framework.

Within the 2006-2015 National Education Plan, the TVET section indicates the government's commitment to: (i) enforce a legislative framework to support the implementation and sustainability of the TVET policy and management systems; (ii) strengthen the institutional capacity of the TVET subsector; and (iii) establish a sound financial basis for TVET's long-term development and sustainability.

The policy prescriptions are to: (i) expand and diversify opportunities for TVET for the increasing numbers of senior secondary leavers; (ii) strengthen the GTTI by introducing higher diploma courses; (iii) create opportunities for workers to upgrade their skills with specially designed courses using ICT and open distance learning, where feasible; (iv) strengthen the NTA to regulate, set standards and certify qualifications; and (v) secure appropriate learning materials from outside the country, while ensuring that other learning materials are locally adapted.

The select strategic interventions are to:

- Encourage employers to facilitate part-time training in TVET for their employees;
- Make TVET programs affordable and accessible and provide scholarships for needy girls;
- Strengthen quality part-time TVET for lifelong learning;
- Develop a comprehensive apprenticeship system for the informal sector;
- Introduce more relevant training programs for rural TVET trainees;
- Reintroduce trade testing and certification;
- Establish the Labor Market Information System;
- Conduct tracer studies;
- Register and accredit trainers and assessors;
- Develop a skills qualification framework;
- Implement the National Education and Technical Training levy;
- Update the national TVET policy; and
- Increase the private sector investment in skills development to 50 percent.

The Training Levy

In the past the government collected a training levy from companies, based on a schedule, and according to companies' size, but the proceeds went to the treasury and were not earmarked for training. The National Education Levy of 1995 was amended in 2005 to collect 0.25 percent of employers' gross annual revenue. Collection started in January 2007 but only lasted a month. Enterprises with high turnover and low profit margins such as banks, were required to pay heavy sums. They resisted and approached the President to present their dilemma, claiming that the levy would cause investors to leave. The President rescinded the law in February 2007 and modified the scheme. The levy introduced in March 2007 now calls for companies earning over D 5 million (US$186,000) to pay a flat fee of D 50,000, and companies earning under D 5 million to pay D 30,000 (US$1,859). There is no lower cutoff point, and therefore all firms are supposed to pay the fee. Seventy five percent of the projected D 7 million (US$260,223) levy revenue goes to the NTA.

The National Training Authority

The NTA, established by Act in 2002, is the lynchpin of TVET reforms. The governing board of the NTA, appointed by the President, includes a chairperson, the Permanent Secretary of the Ministry of Higher Education, Research and Science and Technology, the Permanent Secretary of the Ministry of Finance and Economic Affairs, two private sector representatives, one training institution representative, the Director General of the NTA and the Director of Science and Technology Education. Thus, the government has a majority on the board and labor unions are not represented. The board reports to the Ministry of Higher Education, Research, Science and Technology. In addition, the NTA Act spells out the duties of providers (to provide services which lead to national vocational qualifications) and employers (allow employees the opportunity to obtain national vocational qualifications and undertake ongoing professional development). The section below provides a brief introduction to the main NTA areas of work. Appendix F presents the NTA's functional structure.

The collection of labor market information is one of the NTA's main priorities. This information is used to determine training needs. The LMI section carried out an enterprise training needs assessment survey in 2007 and produced a report that gave a profile of enterprises by sector and indicated the occupations for which enterprises had most difficulty recruiting. The findings indicated skills shortages and recruitment difficulties for marketing, management skills (a reflection of the dominance of retail trade in the survey) and to a lesser extent, technical and trade skills. Currently two studies are underway: a mapping exercise of informal sector master craftsmen, and a survey to list all enterprises with more than five employees, as a basis for arranging internships.

Another of the NTA's main functions is to regulate the provision of training. This role faces criticism from the public due to the lack of value for money offered by many private training providers. The NTA registers and licenses training institutions, trainers and assessors, which places a heavy workload on the institution. Further information on this role is provided in the Effectiveness section below.

Finally, the NTA drafted an apprenticeship policy in July 2006. The aim of the policy is to improve the image and practices of the informal sector, and work-based learning. The objectives are to: (i) strengthen traditional apprenticeship by introducing competency based training and assessment, to link informal skills acquired with the skills framework; (ii) standardize the content, duration, methods, and testing of apprentice certification; (iii) promote technological proficiency and competitiveness; (iv) foster employable skills among low income groups; and (v) create opportunities for further education and training.

The main forms of intervention envisaged are the mapping of master craftsmen, the identification of skills gaps with master craftsmen; the training of trainers, including master craftsmen; and the provision of incentives for participation by informal sector employers. Regional informal sector apprenticeship organizations would be created to drive the process.

Occupational Standards

The Gambian Skills Qualification Framework (GSQF) was introduced in 2006, with preparation assistance from the European Union. The framework consists of: (i) a hierarchy of occupational levels, including a foundation level and four other levels, and (ii) occupational standards that specify the required knowledge and competencies to exercise an occupation. Eventually the GSQF levels will replace the current terminology used, such as certificate and diploma. The adoption of the GSQF promises several benefits, including:

- The focus on outputs/competencies required for performing an occupation;
- The definition of demand-oriented competencies by employers;
- Open access, regardless of prior education;
- The possibility of recognition of prior on-the-job learning;
- The facilitation of assessment and certification through clear performance criteria; and
- The replacement of the need to acquire costly external qualifications, such as City & Guilds.

However, skills qualification frameworks have been problematic in other countries because they tend to be complex, as in South Africa; they are difficult to implement, even in advanced countries - the most successful among them (in Scotland and New Zealand) took 10 to 15 years to develop; and they are difficult and costly to maintain.[10]

In The Gambia, the skills qualification framework is being implemented in the following priority areas:

- Key skills—English, numeracy, work discipline and life skills;
- Tourism;
- Agriculture and horticulture (Levels 1 and 2);
- Motor mechanics, light vehicle maintenance (Level 1; level 2 is underway);
- Electrical installation of buildings (Level 1; level 2 is in process);
- Procurement (Level 1);
- Building, civil works and construction;
- Carpentry;
- Plumbing;
- Road construction and maintenance; and
- Secretarial work.

Occupational standards are developed by panels including employers, sector bodies, trainers and resource persons. Their work is helped by standards already developed in other countries (Jamaica, Botswana, Mauritius and Namibia). Once prepared, the level one and two standards are validated by employers and approved by the NTA board. They are then piloted in training institutions to confirm that they are workable, before being adopted on a larger scale. In the meantime, the panels continue to work on the advanced levels, three and four. Standards will be reviewed every two or three years to keep them up to date with changes in technology.

Occupational standards include the definition of performance criteria. The assessment process uses these criteria to evaluate the acquisition of the required knowledge and skills. The NTA trains and licenses assessors to carry out the assessment process and develop a test question bank.

Analysis of the TVET Sector

Strengths and Weaknesses of TVET

The main Technical and Vocational Education and Training strengths are a sound policy and strategic framework and the existence of a key organization to spearhead reforms, the NTA. Additional strengths include the GTTI, which has a long tradition of skills provision, the extensive provision of TVET by NGOs and CBOs, a widespread system of informal apprenticeships, and the willingness of parents and trainees to pay for training.

The main challenges are the inadequate financing of TVET (and an unsuitable, unsustainable fee system), the lack of tracer studies on labor market outcomes, inadequate opportunities for youth to acquire skills, inadequate coverage in priority areas such as horticulture, the lack of management information about TVET, important gaps in the quality of TVET provision, and insufficient entrepreneurship training.

Moreover, the NTA needs to streamline its system of registration and accreditation, to develop a management information system on training, and to provide support to training institutions on curriculum development. It also needs a skills development fund for the implementation of its programs. Also, the GTTI appears to be relatively isolated from employers and the labor market.

The following analysis assesses the skills development panorama according to the following criteria, each of which is discussed in detail below:

- External efficiency or relevance
- Effectiveness
- Internal efficiency
- Resource mobilization and utilization
- Sustainability

External Efficiency, or Relevance

External efficiency, or relevance, is the relationship between training outputs and objectives on the supply side, and economic and social requirements on the demand side (see Figure 4.6).

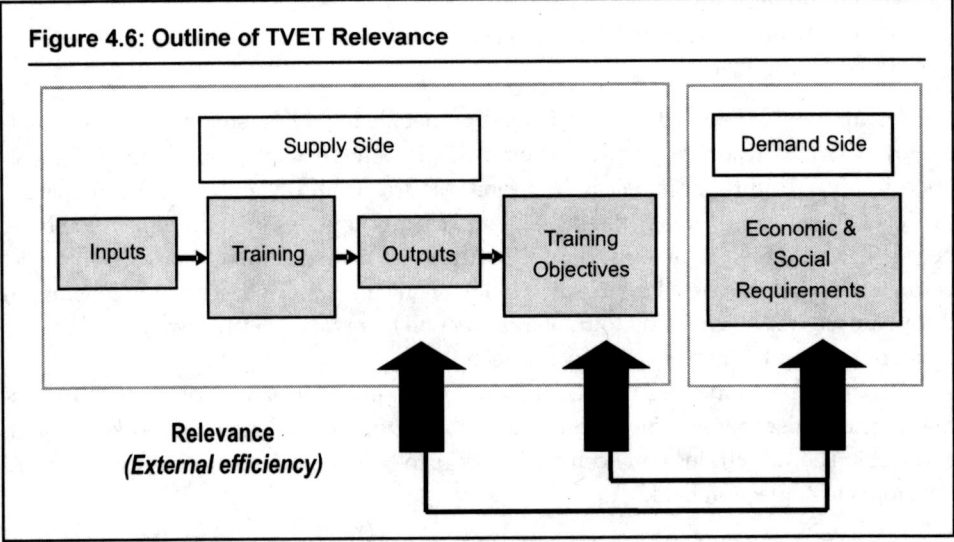

Figure 4.6: Outline of TVET Relevance

Economic Relevance. Some of the critical issues with respect to the economic relevance of TVET are highlighted by the following questions: Is TVET provision relevant to economic requirements? To what extent is the composition of training provision congruent with labor market demands? In other words, to what extent is current TVET provision relevant to the needs of the labor market and employers? The answers to some of these questions are summarized in Table 4.5.

Training for the Informal Sector. Given that the informal sector of the current labor market comprises mainly self-employed workers, especially in agriculture, the extent to which the provision of skills development supports improved productivity in this sector is key. At present it is unclear whether the availability of skills for the agriculture and horticulture sector is sufficient. A mapping exercise would help to establish this. In the mean time, it is worthy of note that one agricultural training center (Njawara) had to delay the start of its new training program for lack of operational funds, and another, (Chamen) is not in operation. The overall level of provision of craft-level skills and training opportunities at the technical level seems to be underdeveloped in relation to demand.

Table 4.5: Economic Relevance of TVET—Strengths and Weaknesses

Strengths	Weaknesses/Challenges
• Training relevance is being improved through: (a) the initiation of labor market analysis under the Labor Market Information section of the NTA, and (b) employer participation in the definition of occupational standards under the new skills qualification framework. • Internships during Year 2 at the GTTI help make the training more practical. • The traditional apprenticeship system is widespread and is probably the main avenue for skills acquisition in the trades. It is closely related to the world of work.	• Employers complain that they cannot find the required quality of skills and work attitudes within the country, so they hire foreigners. • LMIS is still insufficient, meaning that market information is lacking. This is being overcome by the NTA. • Better statistics on work permits by occupation and more tracer studies are required. • Content relevance is weak in terms of the range of subjects offered, multiskilling, and entrepreneurship. • The GTTI lacks links with employers at the board and advisory committees levels. • The NYSS is not very effective in creating employment opportunities for youth. • GTTI staff find it difficult to keep up to date with technological developments.

As noted, training for the informal sector should cover three dimensions which appear to be either missing or inadequately emphasized at present:

1. *Multiskilling.* It is not possible to know in advance exactly what skills will be in demand, and trainees may have to practice different skills at different times. Therefore an exposure to multiple skills would be appropriate;

2. *Wide range of occupations.* The TVET policy noted the limited range of skills taught and the resulting market saturation for some of them. Market analyses need to be conducted in a wider range of occupations that are or are likely to be in demand; then training programs need to be organized accordingly; and

3. *Entrepreneurship.* Most youth entering the labor market will work in the informal sector, often being self-employed, which by definition involves a degree of entrepreneurship. Success requires knowledge and insight into how the market works in terms of pricing goods and services, marketing, quality control, and so on. Training in entrepreneurship consequently needs to be more widespread and delivered through multiple avenues.

Relevant systems of skills development have three characteristics in common: good information about labor market demands; employer involvement in orienting the system; and responsive training providers. Each is discussed below:

1. *Labor Market Information.* Information about market requirements is the first requirement to achieve economic relevance in training provision. The NTA has made an excellent start in forging better links between training and the skills requirements of companies through labor market information gathering and analysis. The NTA has conducted two national assessments of training needs: a household survey in December 2006 and an enterprise survey in 2007. These surveys were followed-up with a report on the "Shortages of Skilled Workers in the Manufacturing Industry." However, little research has been conducted on graduates' labor market outcomes. The most recent data is the result of an NYSS conducted tracer study in 2002, and a GTTI survey in 1996. Lack of tracer information constitutes a major gap in key labor market information. Local market surveys will be as important as national surveys to improve training providers' effectiveness.

2. *Employer Involvement.* Employers need to help steer the TVET system. This is happening through the board and NTA skills definition groups. The NTA links the definition of occupational standards under the GSQF to employer requirements by having a majority of employers constitute its occupational standards working groups.

3. *Responsive Training Providers.* A third requirement for economically relevant skills development is that training providers be responsive. The NTA is expected to play an important role here by providing direction and incentives to training providers. Many training providers tend to offer the same programs year after year because of the inclination to use existing staff and facilities, and without knowledge of labor market outcomes. For example, most training courses appear to be two to three years long; short modular courses can be more flexible but are not offered by most training institutions. Private training providers may be more attune to opportunities for new courses in order to increase their market share.

Social Relevance. Equity of and access to training are key dimensions in terms of achieving social relevance. This section aims to determine the extent to which all ages, income groups, and genders have equal access to training.

Table 4.6: Social Relevance of TVET—Strengths and Weaknesses

Strengths	Weaknesses
• There is relatively good gender equity in private training provision. • Some instances of relevant training exist in agriculture, leading to increased income for rural women (Njawara Agricultural Training College). • NGOs are actively involved in the provision of skills training, including for women. • The NYSS provides opportunities for unemployed youth.	• Overall, relatively few youth have access to organized skills development. • The level of artisan training of female youth is not clear. It is clear that female youth tend to be limited to traditional occupations, for example at the GTTI. • Provincial access to skills development is inadequate. • External exams (City and Guilds) are expensive, meaning that many young people cannot obtain external qualifications.

Equity in access to TVET is examined below (to the extent that data permits), as a whole, and by gender and income group:

1. *Overall Access.* The Gambia has taken strides in providing opportunities for youth to gain occupational skills outside the formal education system. The NYSS has been effective in providing some training to about 200 unemployed youth per year, or 1,500 in total throughout its 12 year existence. However, aggregate access to skills acquisition through organized training remains relatively low, as the population in the 17 to 25 years age group is about 200,000. Of these only about 8,000, or about four percent, have access to organized training programs each year. As a result, it is likely that access to training is particularly weak for artisan skills (compared with technical skills) and in rural areas, but disaggregated statistics are not yet available.

2. *Access by Gender.* Based on information from about 60 training institutions, mostly located in the Banjul area, the distribution of enrollment and output by gender seems to be fairly even. However, these data are biased and do not show the access of female youth to training opportunities in rural areas, where

they may be particularly disadvantaged. Young women tend to take courses in traditionally female occupations that lead to low-income jobs. At the craft level for example, female youth train in sewing, cooking, and secretarial work. At the GTTI on the other hand, where they represent almost 40 percent of enrollment, most train in business studies and IT.

3. *Access by Income.* Low-income youth are doubly disadvantaged; typically they do not have the educational qualifications to follow further education, or the ability to pay private training fees. NGO and CBO support is helpful in providing access to training to lower income groups.

Effectiveness

Effectiveness is defined as the relationship between outputs and education and training objectives (see Figure 4.7). Effectiveness has two dimensions: training effectiveness, or quality, and the effectiveness of TVET organizations and management.

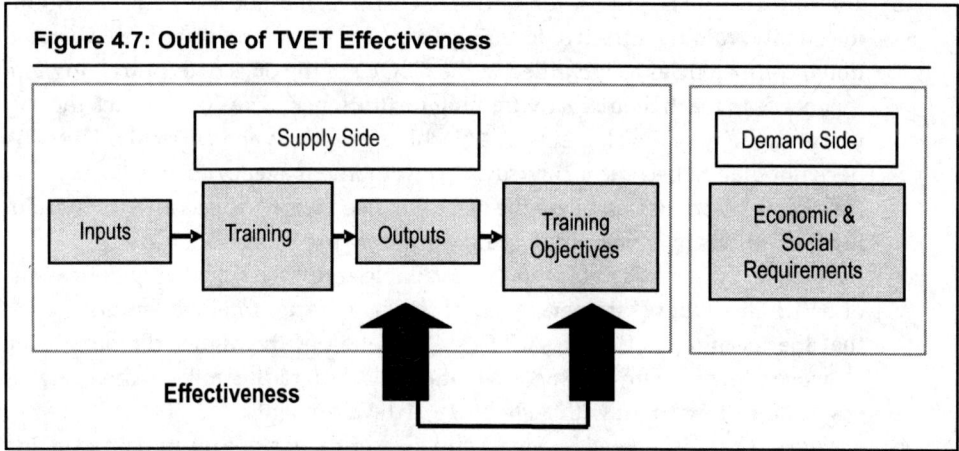

Figure 4.7: Outline of TVET Effectiveness

Training Effectiveness, or Quality. The quality of instruction can be reviewed in terms of inputs, processes, and outputs. This section will offer some elements of response to the following questions: To what extent does TVET provision reach its teaching objectives? How good is the quality of training?

Table 4.7: Quality of TVET Instruction—Strengths and Weaknesses

Strengths	Weaknesses
• Occupational standards have been developed by the NTA for 63 occupations. • Training providers are being registered which should ensure adherence to basic standards. • The NTA is licensing trainers. • The NTA is training assessors and developing assessment and certification procedures. • The GTTI has high pass rates on most of its programs, both internal and external.	• Value for money among private training providers is widely criticized. • The NTA lacks a curriculum development service for teaching to competency based standards. • The NTA may be over regulating training providers and needs to streamline its criteria. • Quality standards in traditional apprenticeship are lacking, and quality varies widely. • The competence and lack of trainers hinders TVET quality. • GTTI equipment and facilities are outdated, with no ready sources for physical or human capital renewal.

The availability of the necessary inputs has a strong influence on the quality of the training process. The main inputs examined here are standards, teaching curricula, instructors, and facilities:

1. *Standards.* The first essential requirement for quality TVET is occupational standards. These are the specification of the outputs required, including the knowledge, skills and competencies needed to practice an occupation. They provide guidance to the training system in terms of content and establish the basis for the evaluation of outputs. Standards should be defined and ratified by employers. The Gambia is making clear progress in defining occupational standards through the NTA, and employers are closely involved. The main advantage is that the GSQF process defined the competencies required to perform an occupation, and clearly specifies the output standards. This varies from typical training programs where achievement is based on time spent (number of months or years in training) rather than the competencies acquired.

2. *Teaching Curricula.* Output standards are essential, but not sufficient, conditions for quality training. Effective teaching programs must also be devised. Occupational competencies as identified in the GSQF are the objectives of training, not the means to reach them. Many training institutions in The Gambia lack the sufficient capacity to develop effective teaching programs and curricula. The NTA does not plan to become a curriculum development agency; that is the work of training institutions. However the NTA will need to provide assistance to training institutions in developing modular training programs.

3. *Instructors.* Systematic data were not available about the teaching qualifications of TVET institutions' trainers, even at the GTTI. Anecdotal evidence suggests that the teaching staff at the GTTI are qualified at the higher diploma level. However, few of them have access to in-service upgrading to keep their knowledge and skills current with technological developments.

4. *Facilities.* There is also widespread criticism of the lack of up-to-date teaching equipment. The 2005/06 Annual Report of the GTTI Engineering Department noted the need for "A replacement plan to be put in place for the archaic capital equipment in the workshops; and procure better equipment to support the rapid transition of the Institute to a Higher Institute of Learning."

Various quality assurance processes have been introduced by the NTA to raise the standards of training achieved. These include the registration and accreditation of training providers, the licensing of trainers, the assessment and certification of trainees, and the development of a staff of assessors:

1. *Registration of Training Providers.* Criticism abounds about low-quality private training providers being driven by greed, preying upon unsuspecting parents and youth, and failing to deliver value for money. The NTA has undertaken to drive out low-quality providers from the market and to ensure basic quality standards through its registration program. Registration is now compulsory to operate in the training provision market.[11] So far about 60 training providers have started or completed the obligatory registration process; another 40 have closed down. Registration criteria are comprehensive, and include: (i) being a legal entity; (ii) having a clear organizational structure; (iii) demonstrating a

clear purpose; (iv) being financially viable; (v) serving learner interest; (vi) being committed to staff development; (vii) having quality management systems; and (viii) safeguarding trainees' records and tuition payments.

2. *Accreditation of Training Providers.* Accreditation is a more advanced, voluntary process that certifies that training providers comply with GSQF standards. It considers additional criteria such as: to have adequate and safe premises, to have developed appropriate training curricula, and to have sufficient and appropriate equipment.

3. *Licensing of Trainers.* The NTA also licenses individual trainers. The Lead Panel checks the credentials of the trainer and interviews prospective trainers to verify their technical competence. Registered training providers are required to employ only licensed trainers.

4. *Assessment and Certification.* The GSQF definition of unit or occupational standards includes specific assessment criteria for testing the acquisition of required knowledge and competencies by students. The NTA is converting these into a test bank. Trainees, once positively assessed, can be certified. The NTA is at present acting as the certifying agency until another organization is developed to assume this function.

5. *Assessor Staff.* NSA is also training and licensing assessors on common assessment practices. Nineteen people were trained as assessors between May and October 2007.

These quality assurance processes should establish minimum training standards. However, the process also imposes a heavy workload on the NTA, with the concomitant staffing implications. The work requires not only the development of systems, but their monitoring, maintenance and updating. The NTA must have a reliable and sufficient flow of income to allow for the staffing and other resources necessary to carry out these functions adequately. The NTA also needs to take care that it does not get overwhelmed by the GSQF, as has happened in other countries (see Young, 2005).

Also, the NTA requires inappropriate information for registration, including some that should be deferred to the accreditation stage, yet excluding some basic requirements, such as curricula, safe premises, and adequate equipment. The registration and accreditation system, as presently conceived, over regulates training providers, in areas such as the quality of management processes, staff development, and financial management. This is both inappropriate (it is not the government's role) and inequitable (no such regulation exists for other private sector enterprises). As such, it may be counterproductive, as these barriers deter legitimate training providers from entering the market.

Few systematic conclusions can be drawn about the quality of training delivered at present because the former testing system has ceased to operate and the new assessment system under the GSQF is just beginning. On the one hand, many observers and practitioners perceive a deterioration in the quality of TVET, in part because of the sector's chronic underfinancing. Some employers complain that graduates do not have the required competencies and therefore hire expatriate workers. For example, some employers in the manufacturing sector questioned the competence of GTTI students and graduates: "The competency of these trainees is below standard. The electrical and mechanical students cannot even read simple electrical and mechanical circuit diagrams.

Students are unable to apply theory to practice."[12] If correct, this indicates a gap in the quality of training.

In this respect, on the one hand only 43 percent of the 1,500 youth trained through the NYSS were employed after their three year training, and only half of those are in the field in which they were trained. A 2002 impact study estimated the costs of training at D 10,800 per student (excluding administrative overheads) and concluded that it was not cost-effective (SIMI Limited, 2003). On the other hand, institutions providing good quality training also exist. These include, among others, SOS Skills Training in Banjul and the Njawara Agricultural Training Center. In addition, the GTTI reports good pass rates of trainees in all sections on their internal examinations, averaging 87 percent. Pass rates are equally good for those who can afford to take the external examinations.[13] Finally, GTTI operation of two new rural training centers should raise the quality of their instruction and outputs.

TVET Organizations and Management. Table 4.8 examines the extent to which key TVET organizations and management reach their objectives.

Table 4.8: TVET Organizational and Management Effectiveness—Strengths and Weaknesses

Strengths	Weaknesses/Challenges
• Sound policy framework and strategy for TVET, the centerpiece of which is the semi-autonomous NTA, established to spearhead TVET reforms, both in terms of relevance and quality. • The NTA appears to be well organized and staffed for its work. • The NTA does not attempt to provide training, which has handicapped national training authorities in other countries.	• Lack of information on the scope and coverage of the skills training system. • The NTA needs to do more to monitor and evaluate the training system, through a management information system for instance. • Skills development is overregulated. Registration could be simplified. • The number of registrations imposes a heavy workload on NTA staff. • Training centers lack the management capacity to carry out essential functions. • The GTTI lacks management information for its operations.

The Gambia has developed a sound policy framework and strategy for TVET reform and has begun to implement it. The main objectives are demand orientation, the establishment of an institutional framework and capacity, and financing reforms. The semi-autonomous NTA is the centerpiece, established to spearhead TVET reforms, both in terms of relevance and quality.

The existence of a national training authority is arguably TVET's single greatest strength. As described above, the NTA is following a logical process to raise the relevance and quality of skills development. It is essentially an intermediary, a development agency for TVET in the country. It is particularly well suited to the atomized structure of training provision in the country where CBOs, NGOs, and private providers dominate.

The NTA is relatively new and appears to be well managed and staffed by competent, enthusiastic professionals. However, the following list provides an indication of areas where it needs to further develop its services:

▪ The labor market information function is critical to shifting training from a supply to a demand orientation. It should be broadened by developing expertise in local market analysis to identify occupations in surplus and demand, and by developing the capacity to carry out tracer studies at the national and institutional levels;

- Training providers will need help in developing curricula and training programs. Occupational standards will not be sufficient;
- Data are lacking at present about training providers and graduates. A full TVET management information system needs to be developed, based in large part on data generated from the registration process; and
- Support for the improvement of training institutions' management should be developed. Some of the objectives are included in the accreditation criteria, and training programs have already been given.

In relation to the last point in particular, although the TVET policy points to weaknesses in training institutions' management to carry out essential functions, no details were provided. No organizational audit of the GTTI was possible or in fact attempted in the course of this review. It is clear, however, that GTTI management lacks a consolidated management information system on its teachers, students, and graduates. For example, the Table 4.2 on GTTI enrollment had to be calculated from information provided by the various sections; no time series data was available for the institution as a whole; nor was any summary of staff by qualifications readily available; detailed information could not be calculated on costs per student or per graduate. A management audit of the GTTI and development of a management information system may be appropriate.

Internal Efficiency

Internal efficiency is defined as the relationship between inputs and outputs (see Figure 4.8). It broadly covers resource mobilization, efficient use of resources and financial sustainability. Each of these areas is discussed below.

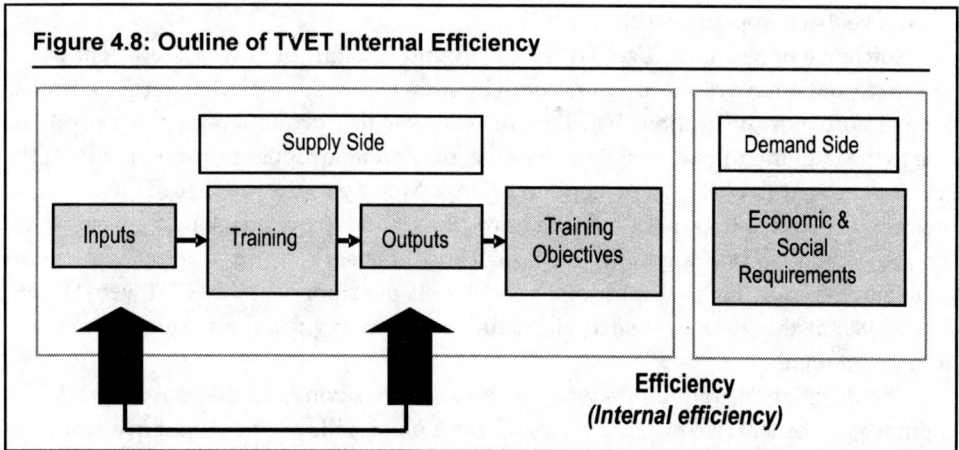

Figure 4.8: Outline of TVET Internal Efficiency

Resource Mobilization. As stated in the TVET policy, the government has traditionally underfinanced TVET. Capital financing has fallen upon donors, particularly the World Bank, but lately most donor aid has focused on providing technical advice. At the time of the development of the TVET policy, government spending on TVET amounted to just four percent of education spending as a whole. Since then, spending priorities have emphasized basic education, so the proportion has fallen even further. For example, government financial support to the GTTI fell from 80 percent of the GTTI's spending in 2000 to just 30 percent in 2005/06.

Table 4.9: TVET Internal Efficiency—Strengths and Weaknesses

Strengths	Weaknesses/Challenges
• The GTTI raises almost 70 percent of its operational expenditures through tuition fees and services. • GTTI recurrent costs per student are low. • GTTI completion rates are high. • Families are apparently willing to pay for skills training, as evidenced by the number of private training providers and fee payments at public institutions. • Traditional apprenticeship costs the government nothing and is self-regulating.	• The NTA has no finance wing to help implement reforms. • The training levy was rescinded on the basis of complaints from businesses; the new schedule penalizes small firms. • Public investment in TVET capacity and upgrading quality is historically below par. • The NYSS programs are not cost-effective. • Training programs may be longer than necessary to teach the stipulated skills. This prevents access to others who need and want training as a result. • The GTTI duplicates the private sector in management, commerce, finance, accountancy, and IT.

The GTTI has generated about 70 percent of its income from tuition fees, and the sale of goods and services. This is an extraordinary accomplishment. It is fueled in large part by the willingness of parents and trainees to pay for training, which has also stimulated the burgeoning private training market, especially in urban areas.

Reforms in the financing of skills development have been problematic and leave an important gap in the system. The second prong of the TVET policy and strategy was the financial framework, the training levy. As discussed, the lack of acceptance of the initial plan led to the reversion to an inequitable system. The system needs to be studied and redesigned as a matter of priority, so that it can offer the capacity to generate sufficient revenue, obtain employers' support, and finance NTA support to training providers. Such a training fund has been strategic in other countries as an instrument to leverage TVET reforms (see Appendix G). The NTA Act makes provision for such a fund, but it has not yet been implemented.

Efficiency of Resource Use. The review found no signs of grossly inefficient use of resources, but not much information could be gathered on the subject. In terms of trainee progression, most institutions had little or relatively low dropout (except for dropouts due to the inability to pay fees). For example, the annual dropout rate of students at the GTTI amounted to only two percent in 2005/06. Moreover, the number of students per instructor appeared to be reasonable in most cases, but data were lacking to provide systematic comparisons. If anything, the issue is not efficient resource use, but constraints on raising revenue. For example, total annual costs per student at the GTTI were D 7,666 or US$380; at this low level such an institution lacks resources for consumables and equipment repair.

The duration of training may be one area where savings could be realized. Many training courses last two or three years, whereas most skills can be taught in a relatively shorter period (that is, a few months of intensive work).[14] Shortening a training program from three to two years could enable an acceleration of output, greater access and a 33 percent reduction in the cost per graduate. The new competency-based training approach inherent in the GSQF does not depend on time spent, but on competencies achieved. Such a system can achieve greater productivity in the use of training resources.

Sustainability. The current TVET system is most likely sustainable, in the sense that most of the financing is by parents and trainees through non government training providers and even government institutions such as the GTTI. However, as stated, the present training levy, which finances the activities of the NTA, is not sustainable under its present form and the NTA risks being deprived of the resources it needs to expand its functions. To its credit, the NTA has devised a schedule of payments for registration and accreditation that will finance its operations in those areas.

Sustaining the GSQF will also be a challenge. As stated, the challenge is to limit the number of occupations covered to keep it within the administrative capability of the NTA. The NTA has taken the wise step of establishing priorities, but it must be vigilant not to allow the skills qualification framework to mushroom into an overly complex program (see Young 2005).

Summary of Recommendations

Counseling services should be provided to potential trainees because youth skills development programs preceded by adequate counseling often have a greater impact and higher chances of success. They also enhance trainees' employability.

Access to skills development programs has gender, economic and geographical biases. Female, poor, and rural youth should receive financial support to acquire skills for employment.

Partnerships between employers and training institutions should be intensified by organizing joint skills training programs with private sector experts, and by providing trainees with opportunities to visit modern factories.

The NTA is the basis of the TVET reform and is well suited to provide direction to the non government providers. There are several areas in which the NTA needs to be strengthened however: (i) to revitalize its Skills Development Fund, which can support the achievement of NTA policy objectives, (ii) to develop the LMIS function, (iii) to provide support in curriculum development to meet new standards under the GSQF, (iv) to simplify the licensing and accreditation requirements, and (v) to ensure that the NTA is made sustainable through recurrent financing.

The GTTI needs additional funding to increase the level and quality of its training. Prior to the additional investment, however, the following activities should be conducted: (i) an academic audit to assess the relevance to industry, (ii) the creation of its management information system, and (iii) the link with employers so that it can develop partnerships with private providers and share training information.

The performance of the NYSS should be improved by: (i) studying successful youth training and employment schemes in other parts of the world, (ii) widening its coverage to include Banjul and more female trainees, (iii) conducting more training in the regions, (iv) paying serious attention to entrepreneurship training and multiskilling, and (v) avoiding the establishment of a NYSS multipurpose training center, instead relying on existing training providers.

Areas for Further Study

Based on the data above, the following key questions warrant further research:

- To what extent is the composition of training provision congruent with labor market demands?
- What levels of skills are over or under provided?
- What types of occupations are over or under trained?
- Are the main constraints on the expansion of the TVET system human, financial, other?

Notes

1. Including management, bookkeeping/accounting, secretarial skills, banking and finance.

2. The board consists of a chairman appointed by the Minister of Education, the Permanent Secretary of the Ministry of Education; the Head of the National Office of the West African Examinations Council, the Permanent Secretary of the Ministry of Trade, Industry and Employment, a representative of the private sector, two NGO representatives, two members of the general public, the GTTI director and a secretary from the GTTI senior management team.

3. The budget was D17.1 million, but the government subsidy was D 1 million short (D 5.1 million instead of the promised D 6.1 million.)

4. GTTI Report, 2001.

5. For example, GTTI staff are building the Sifoe Senior Secondary School under contract with the government.

6. NTA Training Needs Assessment Enterprise Survey, 2007.

7. The Public Expenditure Review of 2006 does not provide data on recurrent expenditures by subsector, only the rates of increase by subsector over several years. Without the base data, the percentage increases are meaningless.

8. PER, 2006. It is not clear whether these figures are current or projections. No comparative data were available on recurrent costs per student or per graduate by type of institution.

9. The projected investment shortfalls were 55 percent for higher education, 83 percent for secondary education and 62 percent for basic education.

10. For a review of international experience with SQFs and their implementation in developing countries, see Young, 2005 and Tuck, 2007.

11. Although no sanctions are specified in the NTA Act for failure to comply with registration standards, sanctions are being developed separately in collaboration with the Ministry of Justice.

12. NTA draft document.

13. Of course, this figure is biased by the natural self-selection process: only those who feel that they will succeed in the external examination are willing to pay the substantial extra costs to sit the test.

14. Dougherty, 1989; Middleton, et al., 1993.

CHAPTER 5

Recommendations

Introduction

In the long term, providing high quality basic education will be paramount in assisting youth to achieve improved employment outcomes. Students will need to master basic math and English skills in order to have a basic foundation upon which to base further skills development and employability. In fact, for low income governments, making sure that children receive a good quality basic education and that they do not drop out is less expensive then establishing training programs to provide youth with second chance opportunities. In addition, there are numerous other policy related interventions that need to be undertaken to encourage employment intensive economic growth. The lack of market opportunities is directly related to the fact that the economic situation remains challenging in that growth is constrained by poor infrastructure and a challenging business climate.

This chapter will focus on steps that can be taken in the short term to address the needs of today's youth. The recommendations in this chapter will be divided into two sections: recommendations at the macro level for policy makers and recommendations at the TVET system level, by type of training. Important steps have been taken over the past few years to improve the TVET system. The following chapter discusses what else should be done by the various TVET stakeholders to strengthen the system.

Recommendations for Policy Makers

Define a better fiscal and monetary policy mix. The Gambia has one of the highest real interest rates in the world, as the Central Bank attempts to keep inflation under control while still issuing domestic debt to cover unanticipated public expenditure. The downside of raising interest rates to counter inflation is that high real interest rates undermine domestic economic activity. Some progress toward renewed fiscal discipline must lay the grounds to reduce real interest rates. Recommended actions include enforcing a hard budget constraint on the operations of state owned enterprises and reducing unnecessary government spending.

Improve the design of the tax system and reduce labor income tax. As a result, this reform should lower the cost of formal job creation. This is important because the single most important nonwage labor cost is labor income taxes, which include the personal income tax and payroll taxes. These taxes discourage labor demand, especially of less skilled workers, further contributing to the slow expansion of formal employment in the economy.

Lower the costs of starting and running businesses. Given that the best opportunity for job creation comes from business start-ups, actions to lower the costs of starting and running businesses would have a high payoff. These actions include: (i) establishing a transparent business environment that is free of undue privileges; (ii) simplifying the tax system; and (iii) setting high standards in public administration services. A structurally deficient public administration increases the cost of regulatory and tax compliance, therefore creating impediments to the development of the private sector as well as to attracting needed foreign direct investment.

Pursue economic policies that stimulate the creation and growth of enterprises and hence the demand for employable skills. Training, even of the highest quality, is not enough to generate employment. Rather, it is the growth of enterprises that creates additional skills needs and opportunities for new jobs. Therefore, whereas training relevance and quality are important in skills development, the economic policy dimension should not be overlooked, as it is necessary to create an enabling environment for business innovation and growth.

Encourage foreign companies to contribute to national skills development efforts. Foreign companies operating in the country can contribute to the development of human capital in the country through the technology transfer process, given that they have the expertise. The government should therefore implement measures to encourage foreign companies to train local workers and enter into training partnerships with local training institutions.

Conduct more in-depth research to better understand how children's employment affects schooling and youth employment outcomes. The degree of child labor in any given country is dependent on the socio-economic climate as well as factors related to culture and access to schooling opportunities. Achieving sustainable reductions in child labor therefore requires a policy response that is cross-sectoral in nature and targets three broad groups: (i) children at risk of involvement in child labor; (ii) children already working; and (iii) children in the worst forms of child labor requiring immediate, remedial action.

Empirical analysis conducted for this study (see Chapter 3) as well as policy experience in The Gambia and elsewhere points to a number of general strategies. Better access to schooling and other basic services, combined with mechanisms to reduce social risk, are particularly important policy responses to prevent children from entering into work, and to stop children already in work from moving to more hazardous forms of labor or leaving school prematurely.

Reduce household vulnerability by expanding social protection. Prevention measures designed to stem the flow of children into work constitute the most important component of a policy response to child labor. Clearly, sustainable reductions in child labor cannot be attained without addressing the factors causing children to enter work in the first place. As children are rarely responsible for their own choices, the design of preventive measures requires an understanding of factors influencing household decisions relating to schooling and work. Empirical results indicate that children's work frequently forms part of households' strategies for dealing with risk, making them less vulnerable to losses of income arising from individual or collective shocks. Widespread poverty and a very limited social protection net imply a very high degree of household vulnerability. A broad range of social protection instruments could be developed, such as conditional cash transfer programs, social pension programs, child grants in severely deprived areas, disability grants, and so on.

Develop remedial education programs and other "second chance" opportunities for children in employment. These are important measures in overcoming work related damage to children's welfare. Second chance education programs offer children who have never enrolled in school, or who have dropped out, a bridge to successful integration or (reintegration) into the formal school system. They are critical to ensure that these children, once back in school, remain there and are able to learn effectively. Programming experience elsewhere points to three main options for offering disadvantaged, unenrolled children opportunities to ease their transition back to school: (i) mainstreaming, or providing returning children and working children with special remedial support within the regular classroom context; (ii) school based catch-up education, involving separate, intensive courses making use of school facilities; and (iii) nonformal bridging education, involving intensive nonformal courses designed to raise academic proficiency.

Promote a supportive national, political, legal, and institutional environment to achieve sustainable reductions in child labor. Political commitment is needed to ensure that child labor is mainstreamed into broader development plans and programs. For example, child labor may be included as an explicit concern in Millennium Development Goals, Education for All plans, and poverty reduction strategy plans. Labor legislation consistent with international child labor standards is necessary both as a statement of national intent and as legal and regulatory framework for efforts against child labor. As child labor is an issue that cuts across sectors and areas of ministerial responsibility, progress against it requires the clear definition of institutional roles, and effective coordination and information sharing.

Correct the levy system, as a matter of urgency. The previous levy system was not working effectively and prompted strong resistance from some sectors, such as banking. The system currently in place penalizes small merchants. As such, one of the pillars of the 2002 TVET policy has not worked. Putting the TVET system on a sound financial footing is a top priority. A study of alternatives and the advantages and feasibility of each should be conducted urgently. Any solution requires close consultation with employers and a consensus on what should be done. (Appendix H presents the terms of reference for such a study).

TVET Level Recommendations

For the NTA, the GTTI, and the NYSS

Strengthen and streamline the NTA. The NTA is the lynchpin of TVET reform. It is developing into a strong organization with a clear purpose. As an intermediary, the NTA is particularly well suited to provide coherence and direction to the dispersed non government training providers that prevail in TVET. The NTA needs to be further strengthened and made sustainable in the following areas:

1. *Set up and finance a skills development fund.* Such a fund is contemplated in the NTA Act, and could be an effective way to stimulate further improvements in the relevance, quality, and efficiency of skills development, particularly among dispersed training providers. This would involve first studying the modus ope-

randi of training funds elsewhere in the region, such as Mauritius. A World Bank review of training funds financed in the Africa region found that linking training funds to national training authorities is effective (see Appendix G). The fund can support the achievement of NTA policy objectives and the NTA can direct funds to priority uses. However, a training fund requires painstaking preparation, including agreement at high policy levels on its rationale, purpose and benefits. Good management and financial autonomy are essential requirements for effectiveness. Balance in the governance structure of a fund is clearly also important; tripartite structures often work well provided that employers have a major voice.

2.   *Manage the NTA's TVET regulatory role in order not to stifle innovation in training provision.* In particular, the adoption of occupational standards by training institutions should not exclude the introduction of new market-driven courses which may fall outside the existing Gambia Skills Qualification Framework. Standardization of training provision should not be misconstrued as uniformity. The NTA should therefore place more emphasis on its accreditation and quality assurance functions than on its other control activities.

3.   *Build the highly valuable LMIS function within the NTA.* This will enable: (i) tracer studies for institutions; and (ii) local market analysis for training centers, particularly in rural areas. These additional functions will require additional staff.

4.   *Map the present system of skills provision and its quantitative dimensions.* This information is essential for planning and guiding the development of skills provision. Valuable statistical information can be collected as a byproduct of the registration process, but thought should be given to the kind of information needed for management purposes and how to update it regularly.

5.   *Provide help in curriculum development and instructor training to meet new standards under the GSQF.* As stated, it is not the job of the NTA to develop teaching programs for training providers; however, most of the providers do not have the capacity to do so themselves and need assistance in developing modular programs. The NTA has started to provide this help and its future plans call for the pursuit of efforts in this direction.

6.   *Simplify licensing and accreditation requirements, focusing on basic minimum standards at the initial licensing stage.* These minimum standards should protect the public from exploitation, and include standards for adequate and safe facilities; appropriate equipment in working order; appropriate content; trained teachers and the safeguard of student fee payments. Accreditation requirements can then focus on quality assurance processes.

7.   *Ensure NTA sustainability.* The NTA must be financially sustainable, receiving the recurrent financing it needs to carry out its seminal functions. Also, caution and restraint should be exercised in scaling up the GSQF. Existing occupational profiles should be fully developed, tested and revised before developing new occupational standards. Otherwise, rapid expansion could make the SQF unmanageable, as has happened in other countries.[1]

Increase investment in the GTTI to raise the level and quality of its training. The GTTI has a continuing lead role to play in the delivery of technical and vocational skills. However, before additional investment occurs, the following activities should be undertaken:

- Conduct an academic audit of the GTTI;
- Build its management information system;
- Build better links between the GTTI and employers;
- The GTTI should consider partnerships with private training providers to avoid duplicating training in low-cost fields. the GTTI should instead concentrate on areas that private providers are not willing to cover (high-cost technical fields); and
- Invest in curricula development, new and replacement equipment, and especially in-service staff development.

Review and strengthen NYSS performance by learning from successful youth training and employment schemes in Africa. The following actions could be undertaken:

- Include Banjul and more female trainees in the NYSS;
- Rely on rigorous market analysis and tracer studies (by the NTA);
- Include multiskilling;
- Pay serious attention to entrepreneurship training;
- Provide placement assistance, microcredit and mentoring; and
- Avoid establishing an NYSS multipurpose training center; instead, rely on other training providers, but make financing conditional on performance.

For Public and Private Training Providers

Intensify partnerships between training providers and employers. The report examines the importance of the voice of employers in skills development in some detail. Indeed the most effective dialogue between training and employment is in the area of partnership. Partnerships can take the form of joint skills training programs, use of part-time industry based experts as key advisors and instructors, and access to modern factory equipment by learners in pre employment training programs. Innovative partnerships between training institutions and the private sector can lead to greater relevance, quality, and cost-effectiveness in training delivery.

Continuously update the professional and pedagogical skills of TVET instructors and system managers. The skills training programs covered by the study are overwhelmingly in traditional occupational areas, commerce, and IT, for over one third of the total. There is evidence that the job market in the services sector is shrinking, a situation which calls for the diversification of skills training. This requires expertise in pedagogy and curriculum development. There is therefore the need to upgrade the pedagogical and professional skills of TVET teachers and system managers to enable them to respond to the challenge of designing new training programs and strengthening existing ones.

Increase the use of technology and modern farm practices in the agricultural sector. The agricultural sector employs the largest number of workers. However, the sector still operates at the subsistence level, and its productivity is declining. The infusion of modern farm practices and technology into the sector can help increase productivity and the demand for employable skills in areas such as food preservation and agro-processing, maintenance and repair of farm machinery, and the fabrication of simple agricultural tools. Extending technology to rural areas can also contribute to stemming the rural to urban migration.

Take globalization into account in skills development strategies. The process of globalization and liberalization of international markets can undermine the competitiveness of indigenous goods and services, even on the domestic market. Indeed, in struggling economies, locally produced goods may be more expensive than similar imported goods. Skills development strategies should therefore target productive sectors where the country has a competitive advantage.

Incorporate a life-long learning element in skills development strategies. The rapid advances and changes in technology in the work place mean that the skills and competencies of workers constantly need updating. Life-long learning has therefore become a major component of skills development strategies. Learning critical skills such as creative thinking, problem-solving and team-work is a prerequisite for reskilling, upskilling and multiskilling. Systems for the validation of prior learning, and national skills qualification frameworks also encourage life-long learning. The NTA should therefore be supported to complete its work in progress on the Gambia Skills Qualification Framework.

Provide counseling services prior to and in parallel with youth skills development programs. Youth skills development programs preceded by adequate counseling of potential trainees often have greater impact and higher chances of success for trainees, and enhance their employability. This is important given that employability is the key goal of skills training.

Emphasize gender, equity, and access dimensions in training. Access to skills development programs not only has a gender bias but also economic and geographical biases. Youth from poor households and rural backgrounds and female youth in particular should therefore be financially supported to acquire productive skills for employment.

Develop a specific strategy for the acquisition of skills by female youth. Traditional apprenticeship mostly excludes female youth. They may also be neglected by current training provision at the artisan level (except those with Grade 12 qualifications in urban areas). It is clear that young women tend to be placed in traditional occupations with low income generating potential. Consequently, more analysis is needed to identify potential occupations (demand constraints) and the nature and extent of the underprovision of training to female youth (supply constraints) in order to determine appropriate remedies.

The conditions that make training effective are the same for women as they are for men: jobs must be available, and good links must be forged between training institutions and employers to ensure that training is relevant to market needs. But these conditions are not sufficient to enhance employment opportunities for women.[2] As stated, the status and pay of the jobs for which most women are prepared are comparatively low. However, targeted training that heavily involves employers can help women enter higher-paying, nontraditional programs. Special programs to channel women into nontraditional occupations have been successful in countries as diverse as Morocco, Jamaica and Chile. Key factors in the success of these programs included employer commitment to hire women, extensive publicity campaigns, strong counseling and placement services, the recruitment of female instructors and staff commitment to training women for these nontraditional occupations.[3]

For the Informal Sector

Include entrepreneurship in all training programs. Entrepreneurship should be introduced in the traditional school system and taught intensively in all skills development programs. The subject should be taught by entrepreneurs, not educators. The structure of the labor market provides clear justification for this priority. Youth who want to be self-employed and start their own business should also be provided with an array of complementary support services (for example information about the business registration process, information and access to credit, etc).

Take *the following* **elements into account for successful entrepreneurship training:**

- Include market analysis and feasibility studies, to identify productive occupations. For greater success, these should be offered by locality;
- Carefully select trainees who have the motivation and ability to succeed. Not everyone is suited to be an entrepreneur;
- Offer effective vocational/technical training that meets set standards. This training should also include multiskilling as it is not always possible to know in advance what areas jobs will be available, and many jobs involve a variety of skills;
- Make entrepreneurship training intensive and practical, including visits to small businesses, internships, and the preparation of business plans. The International Labour Organization programs Start Your Business and Improve Your Business could be most useful;
- Follow up on assistance and microcredit and offer continuous mentoring; and
- Carry out local tracer studies to identify market saturation or continued demand, as a basis for adjusting training provision.

Use local market surveys to identify a wider range of occupations in demand and diversify training programs, targeting priority economic sectors such as agriculture and construction. Successful programs should be replicated, especially in horticulture, such as that of the Njawara Agricultural Training Center. Good examples exist of successful training programs that lead to increased income for graduate trainees. The management of these institutions could take over that of other similar training institutions, or provide mentoring.

Suggestions of Further Potential Training Programs

Develop training for the construction sector. Construction, along with tourism, is one of the employment growth sectors. In construction, where many non Gambians are employed, a case could be made for a special effort to encourage the replacement of foreign workers. Construction skills are often best learned on the job, or after a short pre service training course. The NTA could design a training program in close collaboration with contractors, that could include: (i) initial modular training in occupations deemed critical by the contractors; and (ii) wage or other subsidies to encourage contractors to hire Gambian apprentices. The effectiveness of the program would have to undergo careful review.

Study whether additional training supply capacity needs to be built at the artisan and technician levels. The study should cover the specific fields where the requirement may exist, and alternatives such as the intensification of existing capacity, the division of labor with private training providers, training abroad, and so on.

Hotel and tourism training. The management of the Hotel School should be turned over to the Gambia Hotel Association or to a board composed of industry representatives. Demand for graduates is strong, and expanded pre service provision would be justified based on tracer studies of past graduates and industry estimates of demand. The Hotel School could provide more short, targeted in-service training courses for the industry, especially during the lengthy low season.

Community skills training. Successful examples of community skills training exist, such as that operated by Community Skills Development Centers in Namibia, or the Proyecto Joven in Chile and Argentina. Under this "Youth Projects" approach, prospective training providers identify skills in demand, recruit unemployed youth, compete for funds to provide the training, and are paid on the basis of the number of youth that successfully complete the training and are placed in employment (or internships). This approach, of course, requires the existence of a fairly advanced enterprise structure.[4]

For the Traditional Apprenticeship System

Develop a strategy to raise the quality of traditional apprenticeships. This study asserts that traditional apprenticeship is probably the principal means of skills acquisition by male youth. The NTA has developed an apprenticeship policy, which is a useful start. Now a strategy including objectives, resources and actions must be developed to raise the quality of traditional apprenticeships. Gambian authorities should study regional experiences (previous World Bank studies are rich with examples and lessons).[5]

The process of upgrading traditional apprenticeship training could be summarized as follows: (i) identify the occupations with the best prospects; (ii) identify the best artisans and mentors, using the results of the NTA mapping study; (iii) provide master craftsmen with training; (iv) subsidize the training of youth under master craftsmen on a per trainee basis (or some other incentive); and (v) monitor, assess and certify the graduates. Also prepare exit strategies for each trainee, in terms of job placement, access to microfinancing for self-employment, mentoring, and so on. Generally, there are four ways to support traditional apprenticeships. They include:

1. *Upgrading the skills of master craftsmen.* Master craftsmen are the key trainers of all informal sector workers. It is thus important that they are kept abreast of new and appropriate technologies. In addition to technical skills, there is an almost universal need for training in entrepreneurial, cost estimation and accounting skills. Several projects have supported the upgrading of master craftsmen, including Kenya SITE, Uganda UNIDO, and Cameroon APME.

2. *Providing complementary training for apprentices.* The training of apprentices in the informal sector is typically unorganized, often haphazard and provided with highly variable levels of expertise. One way to compensate this is to provide additional training before, outside, or after the apprenticeships. Several projects have adopted this approach, including Benin BAA and Zimbabwe ISTARN.

3. *Work through informal sector associations.* Reaching employers and apprentices in the informal sector can be complicated by the lack of registration and structure of businesses. In many countries artisan associations exist to build members' capacities, including through training. Using these associations can facilitate the delivery and improvement of training services.

4. *Promote supply side initiatives to generate demand responses.* The idea here is essentially to provide financing directly to trainees through voucher programs. Vouchers are intended to introduce consumer choice, enabling informal sector workers to purchase the training they want from a range of approved providers. The availability of financing would then generate a supply response, the emergence, or growth of training providers.

For the Private Sector (Employers)

Provide more labor market information. The functioning of the formal labor market can be affected by the circulation of information on job availability. In The Gambia, public announcements or advertisements for vacant or opening jobs are very scarce. Firms use sources of information like friends, current employees, or relatives to identify candidates. This may negatively affect the matching of labor supply and demand as these informal social networks do not guarantee that the information collected is neutral and truthfully reflects job seekers' actual skills. However, given that the majority of jobs are found through social networks, it is worth considering how to help youth tap into social networks to which they might not necessarily have access, especially higher skilled youth in urban areas. Networking events have proven effective in other countries, mostly Western, and might be an approach worth considering.

Give young people information on skills in demand and sectors that will experience growth in the future. This will enable them to make informed decisions about skills training opportunities.

Notes

1. Young, 2005.
2. Middleton, et al., 1993.
3. Middleton, et al., 1993.
4. Castro, 1999, and Castro et al., 1998.
5. Johanson and Adams, 2006 includes two sets of country studies, for West and Central Africa.

Appendixes

Appendix A: Computation of Sampling Weights for The Gambia Household Surveys

Purpose

The 2008 Gambia household survey is divided into urban and rural sections, each with different sampling processes. The aim was to compute appropriate sampling weights. It was carried out for the following samples:

- The rural section, covering households from the CDDP project from villages among the two poorest thirds of each ward.
- The urban section, covering households already surveyed in the 2003 integrated household survey.
- The country representative sample, combining both.

In addition, we conducted a comparison of various statistics of the latter sample to check the validity of the database as a representative sample of The Gambia.

Harmonization of Sampling Weights to Obtain a Representative Sample

New weights for the rural section of the survey were computed according to the following decisions:

- To keep several sampled villages from the two wards in each local government area (LGA), adjusting the weights according to the third solution suggested in the following section and its assumptions. Hypothesis R and Hypothesis S were both retained.

- To maintain the existing weights for villages other than the two wealthiest in each ward. For these, to overweight the previous weights according to the number of rich villages in the ward that were excluded, using the following formula:

For the richest village of the ward:

$$\frac{2}{3}\left(\frac{2}{NB\_Wards\_in\_LGA\_k} \times \frac{1}{NB\_rich\_villages\_in\_ward\_k} \times \frac{NB\_surveyed\_HH\_in\_village\_j}{NB\_HH\_in\_village\_j}\right)^{-1}$$

For the 2nd richest village of the ward:

$$\frac{1}{3}\left(\frac{2}{NB\_Wards\_in\_LGA\_k} \times \frac{1}{NB\_rich\_villages\_in\_ward\_k} \times \frac{NB\_surveyed\_HH\_in\_village\_j}{NB\_HH\_in\_village\_j}\right)^{-1}$$

- To select the two richest wards in order to reduce potential noise. Otherwise, all rich villages would have been represented by only 12 villages.
- To append the new rural weights to the weights for urban households and obtain a set of harmonized sampling weights representing The Gambia as a whole.

Comparison of Basic Statistics with the 2003 Integrated Household Survey

Apart from the 2008 survey, the most recent Gambian household survey dates back to 2003. Given the time elapsed between surveys, we only conducted comparison with variables that are more or less stable through time: ethnicity, population distribution across local government areas and education.[1] We elaborated a series of bar graphs comparing the 2003 weighted statistics with the 2008 statistics, using 2 different sets of harmonized weights (for hypotheses R and S), and no weights.

We found that using weights for the 2008 household survey leads to major changes in most statistics. Using weights for computing ethnicity statistics gives acceptable results only for the most common ethnic groups. The choice of hypothesis R or S only changes results at the margin. We cannot make any recommendations as to which one is most appropriate.

The following graphs display the results for each comparison:

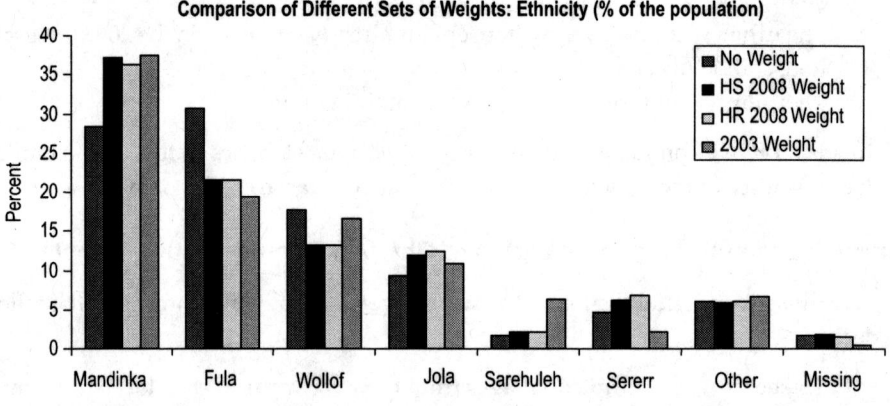

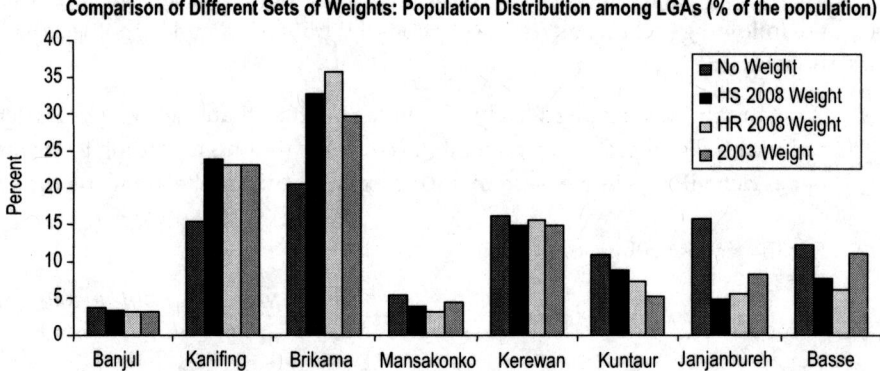

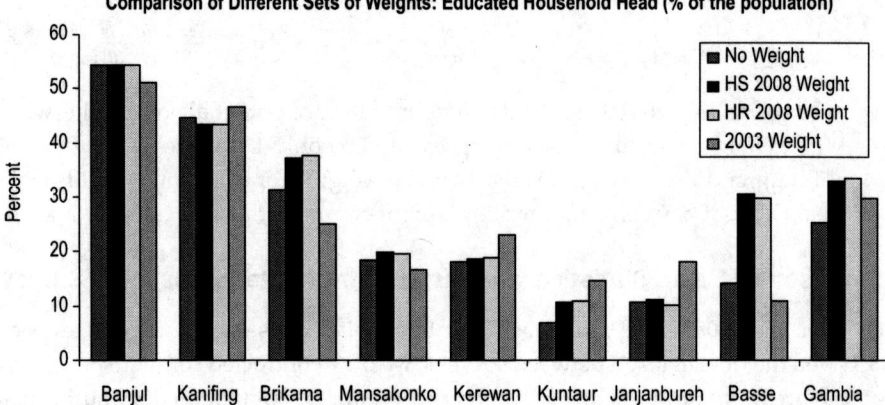

Methodology used in the CDDP survey sampling process

The CDDP survey carried out the random selection of two wards for each LGA, of a total of 12 to 24 wards per LGA. Two wards could be representative of all wards in a LGA, unless the wards are very diverse. To check this, we compared the average population of the two sampled wards with the average population of all wards in each LGA. For Brikama, Kerewan and Kuntaur, sampled wards are much larger than average, leading to a significant upward bias on the estimated LGA population.[2] We discarded the possibility of correcting the weights to obtain correct population figures because biases would remain or even increase in other dimensions.[3] In this context, two wards are simply not a representative sample of all wards in a given LGA.

LGA	Average Size of the 2 Sampled Wards	Average Size of the LGA Wards	Estimated Population of Eligible Villages	Exact Population of Eligible Villages	Number of Wards
Basse	4,750	5,400	66,000	75,449	14
Brikama	12,900	7,100	310,000	163,046	24
Janjanburay	3,750	3,400	45,000	56,309	12
Kerewan	8,050	5,400	130,000	83,271	10
Kuntaur	7,850	4,400	78,000	44,482	16
Mansakonko	3,000	3,000	36,000	35,822	12

This issue means that the sample does not include rich villages. However, biases for the whole population and biases at the LGA level tend to compensate for each other to some degree. Moreover, the fewer wards there are in an LGA, the smaller the bias for this LGA will be.

Conclusion

Sample weights for the urban section of the survey seem to be reliable. For the rural section, there is some evidence that the sample selection is slightly biased at the LGA level, but biases at the country level are less significant. Given that this survey structurally excludes rich villages, they had to be simulated through the computing of harmonized weights.

Notes

1. A reliable age variable was not available for the 2003 survey.
2. These biases could also be explained by a biased estimation of the population of the sampled wards. However we checked that the population of sampled wards was correctly estimated. The bias is not surprising given the number of villages in each sampled ward.
3. For instance, this modification would not change the Educated Household Head graph.

Appendix B: Determinants of Children's Employment and Schooling

Appendix Table B.1: Marginal Effect of Determinants of Children's Employment and Schooling, by Type of Activity, According to Biprobit Estimations, 2008 RY

Explanatory Variables		Only in Employment		Only Schooling		Both Activities		Neither Activity	
		dy/dx	Z	dy/dx	Z	dy/dx	Z	dy/dx	z
Child Age and Gender	Age	-0.0748	-3.7	0.0742	2.1	0.1179	3.6	-0.1172	-5.2
	Age Squared	0.0035	3.7	-0.0037	-2.2	-0.0049	-3.2	0.0051	4.8
	Male	0.0270	3.1	-0.0660	-4.3	0.0603	4.2	-0.0213	-2.2
Household Characteristics	Ln Household Expenditure	-0.0164	-2.4	0.0177	1.5	0.0222	2.0	-0.0235	-3.0
	Access to Piped Water	-0.0407	-3.9	0.0561	2.9	0.0241	1.3	-0.0395	-3.3
	Household Size	-0.0040	-3.0	0.0054	2.3	0.0027	1.3	-0.0040	-2.8
	Number of Children Aged 0-4	0.0064	1.7	0.0006	0.1	-0.0282	-4.7	0.0212	5.2
	Number of Children Aged 5-14	0.0220	7.3	-0.0349	-6.6	-0.0001	0.0	0.0130	3.9
	Male Household Head	0.0586	5.2	-0.1046	-4.0	0.0031	0.1	0.0430	2.7
Education of Household Head	Primary	-0.0639	-5.0	0.1453	4.3	-0.0637	-2.2	-0.0178	-0.8
	Secondary	-0.0755	-6.4	0.0824	2.9	0.0878	3.2	-0.0947	-7.2
	Higher*	-0.0884	-6.9	0.1739	3.8	-0.0057	-0.1	-0.0798	-4.2
Residence and Local Government Area	Urban	-0.0635	-5.0	0.1376	5.5	-0.0824	-3.8	0.0083	0.5
	Banjul	-0.1178	-12.8	0.3582	7.9	-0.1636	-4.3	-0.0768	-2.9
	Kanifing	-0.1174	-10.6	0.3004	8.8	-0.1457	-5.3	-0.0374	-1.8
	Brikama	-0.1270	-12.6	0.2821	10.6	-0.0944	-4.0	-0.0607	-4.1
	Mansakonko	-0.0896	-7.7	0.1986	4.9	-0.0421	-1.1	-0.0669	-3.3
	Kerewan	-0.0241	-1.8	0.0018	0.1	0.0789	2.8	-0.0566	-3.9
	Kuntaur	-0.0303	-2.0	0.0772	2.4	-0.0756	-2.7	0.0287	1.3
	Janjanbureh	-0.0125	-0.8	0.0029	0.1	0.0397	1.4	-0.0301	-1.8

Source: UCW calculations based on the Gambia Joint Rural Labour Force/CDDP Baseline Survey, 2008.
Note: The reference categories are female gender, no education of household head; Basse LGA, and rural area. * The higher education category includes vocational postsecondary schools, colleges, post O-Level vocational and technical schools, universities, and master and PhD. programs.

Appendix Table B.2: Marginal Effect of Determinants of Children's Employment and Schooling in Urban Areas, by Type of Activity, According to Biprobit Estimations, 2008 RY

Explanatory Variables		Only in Employment		Only Schooling		Both Activities		Neither Activity	
		dy/dx	Z	dy/dx	Z	dy/dx	Z	dy/dx	z
Child Age and Gender	Age	-0.0297	-1.9	0.0938	1.5	-0.0070	-0.1	-0.0570	-1.9
	Age Squared	0.0014	1.9	-0.0044	-1.5	0.0005	0.2	0.0026	1.8
	Male	-0.0058	-0.9	0.0052	0.2	0.0233	1.0	-0.0226	-1.7
Household Characteristics	Ln Household Expenditure	-0.0184	-3.2	0.0292	1.3	0.0496	2.7	-0.0604	-5.2
	Access to Piped Water	-0.0174	-1.8	0.0719	2.1	-0.0420	-1.4	-0.0125	-0.7
	Household Size	-0.0004	-0.5	0.0019	0.5	-0.0012	-0.4	-0.0003	-0.2
	Number of Children Aged 0-4	-0.0037	-1.2	0.0250	2.0	-0.0256	-2.3	0.0043	0.7
	Number of Children Aged 5-14	0.0069	2.7	-0.0275	-2.7	0.0123	1.4	0.0083	1.6
	Male Household Head	0.0214	3.1	-0.1172	-3.4	0.0835	2.9	0.0123	0.7
Education of Household Head	Primary	-0.0197	-2.4	0.0873	2.0	-0.0370	-0.9	-0.0306	-1.5
	Secondary	-0.0287	-4.3	0.0671	1.9	0.0328	1.1	-0.0712	-5.2
	Higher*	-0.0326	-4.4	0.0475	0.8	0.0659	1.1	-0.0808	-6.3
Residence and Local Government Area	Urban	-0.0400	-5.9	0.2574	6.8	-0.1679	-5.6	-0.0495	-2.3
	Banjul	-0.0485	-3.9	0.2514	5.5	-0.1936	-5.2	-0.0092	-0.4
	Kanifing	-0.0275	-3.0	0.1564	3.4	-0.1187	-3.3	-0.0102	-0.4
	Brikama	-0.0020	-0.1	0.0338	0.4	-0.0981	-1.7	0.0662	1.0
	Mansakonko	-0.0175	-1.7	0.0457	0.8	0.0135	0.3	-0.0417	-2.0
	Kerewan	-0.0306	-4.0	0.2045	3.3	-0.1436	-2.7	-0.0302	-0.8
	Kuntaur	-0.0314	-4.2	0.1483	2.3	-0.0528	-0.8	-0.0641	-3.0

Source: UCW calculations based on the Gambia Joint Rural Labour Force/CDDP Baseline Survey, 2008.
Note: The reference categories are female gender, no education of household head; Basse LGA. * The higher education category includes vocational postsecondary schools, colleges, post O-Level vocational and technical schools, universities, and master and PhD. programs.

Appendix Table B.3: Marginal Effect of Determinants of Children's Employment and Schooling in Rural Areas, by Type of Activity, According to Biprobit Estimations, 2008 RY

Explanatory Variables		Only in Employment		Only Schooling		Both Activities		Neither Activity	
		dy/dx	Z	dy/dx	Z	dy/dx	Z	dy/dx	z
Child Age and Gender	Age	-0.1065	-3.3	0.0636	1.7	0.1774	4.5	-0.1345	-4.7
	Age Squared	0.0051	3.2	-0.0033	-1.9	-0.0075	-3.9	0.0058	4.2
	Male	0.0598	4.2	-0.0842	-5.2	0.0560	3.2	-0.0316	-2.6
Household Characteristics	Ln Household Expenditure	-0.0116	-1.1	0.0123	1.0	0.0022	0.2	-0.0028	-0.3
	Access to Piped Water	-0.0336	-1.9	0.0154	0.7	0.0632	2.6	-0.0450	-3.0
	Household Size	-0.0072	-3.3	0.0059	2.3	0.0070	2.7	-0.0056	-3.0
	Number of Children Aged 0-4	0.0154	2.6	-0.0060	-0.9	-0.0356	-5.1	0.0263	5.3
	Number of Children Aged 5-14	0.0298	6.4	-0.0300	-5.5	-0.0108	-1.9	0.0110	2.7
	Male Household Head	0.0835	4.0	-0.0680	-2.2	-0.0821	-2.2	0.0666	3.3
Education of Household Head	Primary	-0.0908	-3.6	0.1408	3.2	-0.0650	-1.7	0.0150	0.5
	Secondary	-0.0866	-3.1	0.0376	1.0	0.1409	3.2	-0.0919	-4.6
	Higher*	-0.1415	-5.9	0.2387	4.0	-0.0637	-1.4	-0.0336	-1.0
Residence and Local Government Area	Brikama	-0.2171	-13.4	0.3235	10.1	-0.0504	-1.7	-0.0559	-3.0
	Mansakonko	-0.1611	-9.1	0.2400	5.1	0.0025	0.1	-0.0814	-3.4
	Kerewan	-0.0319	-1.5	-0.0046	-0.2	0.1052	3.4	-0.0687	-3.9
	Kuntaur	-0.0379	-1.6	0.0585	1.9	-0.0474	-1.5	0.0269	1.1
	Janjanbureh	-0.0147	-0.6	-0.0040	-0.2	0.0573	1.8	-0.0387	-2.0

Source: UCW calculations based on the Gambia Joint Rural Labour Force/CDDP Baseline Survey, 2008.
Note: The reference categories are no education of household head; Basse LGA. * The higher education category includes vocational postsecondary schools, colleges, post O-Level vocational and technical schools, universities, and master and PhD. programs.

Appendix Table B.4: Marginal Youth Employment Probability Effects, 2008 RY

Explanatory Variables		dy/dx	Z
Youth Age, Gender and Education	Age	0.1668	3.1
	Age Squared	-0.0034	-2.5
	Male	0.0770	4.0
	Primary	-0.1161	-4.0
	Secondary	-0.1752	-7.3
	Higher*	-0.2240	-8.5
Household Characteristics	Ln Household Expenditure	-0.0276	-2.0
	Access to Piped Water	-0.0952	-4.4
	Household Size	0.0079	3.2
	Number of Children Aged 0-4	0.0299	3.8
	Number of Children Aged 5-14	-0.0022	-0.4
	Male Household Head	0.0071	0.3
Residence	Urban	0.0759	2.8
Local Labor Market Variables	Labor Demand**	2.4967	21.7
	Labor Supply***	0.1123	1.0

Source: UCW calculations based on the Gambia Joint Rural Labour Force/CDDP Baseline Survey, 2008.
Note: The reference categories are female gender, no education of household head; rural area. * The higher education category includes vocational postsecondary schools, colleges, post O-Level vocational and technical schools, universities, and master and PhD. programs. ** Labor demand is proxied by the prime age employment to population ratio. *** Labor supply is proxied by the youth to prime age population ratio.

Appendix Table B.5: Marginal Youth Employment Probability Effects, by Level of Education, 2008 RY

Explanatory Variables		No Schooling		Primary		Secondary		Higher[a]	
		dy/dx	z	dy/dx	z	dy/dx	z	dy/dx	z
Youth Age and Gender	Age	0.2230	3.1	0.3391	2.5	0.0104	0.1	-0.0773	-0.6
	Age Squared	-0.0053	-2.8	-0.0078	-2.2	0.0009	0.4	0.0024	0.8
	Male	0.0138	0.5	0.1367	2.8	0.1106	3.5	0.0398	1.2
Household Characteristics	Ln Household Expenditure	-0.0241	-1.2	0.0306	0.9	-0.0550	-2.2	-0.0388	-1.6
	Access to Piped Water	-0.0229	-0.7	-0.1349	-2.3	-0.1148	-3.2	-0.0819	-1.9
	Household Size	0.0109	3.0	0.0007	0.1	0.0054	1.3	0.0090	2.3
	Number of Children Aged 0-4	0.0179	1.7	0.0185	0.9	0.0536	3.8	0.0070	0.4
	Number of Children Aged 5-14	-0.0008	-0.1	0.0073	0.5	0.0014	0.1	-0.0215	-1.9
	Male Household Head	0.0952	1.6	-0.0246	-0.3	-0.0944	-2.1	0.0883	2.0
Residence	Urban	-0.0403	-0.9	0.1041	1.4	0.1439	3.4	0.0725	1.6
Local Labor Market Variables	Labor Demand**	2.0332	12.2	2.9044	9.4	2.1580	11.2	1.9089	10.1
	Labor Supply***	0.1631	0.9	0.4149	1.4	0.1346	0.7	-0.2213	-1.1

Source: UCW calculations based on the Gambia Joint Rural Labour Force/CDDP Baseline Survey, 2008.
Note: The reference categories are female gender, no education of household head; rural area.* The higher education category includes vocational postsecondary schools, colleges, post O-Level vocational and technical schools, universities, and master and PhD. programs.** Labor demand is proxied by the prime age employment to population ratio. *** Labor supply is proxied by the youth to prime age population ratio.

Appendix Table B.6: Marginal Youth Employment Probability Effects, by Area of Residence, 2008 RY

Explanatory variables		Urban		Rural	
		dy/dx	z	dy/dx	z
Youth Age, Gender and Education	Age	0.1021	1.6	0.1945	3.2
	Age Squared	-0.0018	-1.1	-0.0044	-2.7
	Male	0.0370	1.6	0.0753	3.5
	Ln Household Expenditure	0.0062	0.1	-0.1411	-4.1
	Access to Piped Water	-0.0091	-0.3	-0.2168	-7.2
	Household Size	-0.0744	-2.3	-0.2743	-6.7
Household Characteristics	Number of Children Aged 0-4	-0.0020	-0.1	-0.0511	-3.0
	Number of Children Aged 5-14	-0.0766	-2.5	-0.0443	-1.7
	Male Household Head	0.0039	1.5	0.0088	2.8
	Urban	0.0219	2.2	0.0241	2.6
	Labor Demand**	-0.0039	-0.5	0.0007	0.1
	Labor Supply***	0.0026	0.1	0.0156	0.4
Local Labor Market Variables	Labor demand**	1.6092	12.2	2.7287	16.5
	Labor supply***	0.1997	1.5	0.5576	3.4

Source: UCW calculations based on the Gambia Joint Rural Labour Force/CDDP Baseline Survey, 2008.
Note: The reference categories are female gender, no education of household head; rural area.* The higher education category includes vocational postsecondary schools, colleges, post O-Level vocational and technical schools, universities, and master and PhD. programs. ** Labor demand is proxied by the prime age employment to population ratio. *** Labor supply is proxied by the youth to prime age population ratio.

Appendix Table B.7: Marginal Youth Employment Probability Effects, for Urban Areas, by Level of Education, 2008 RY

Explanatory variables		No Schooling		Primary		Secondary		Higher*	
		dy/dx	z	dy/dx	Z	dy/dx	z	dy/dx	z
Youth Age and Gender	Age	0.6299	3.5	0.0848	0.5	-0.0077	-0.1	-0.1178	-0.9
	Age Squared	-0.0148	-3.3	-0.0014	-0.3	0.0013	0.5	0.0033	1.0
	Male	0.0800	1.2	0.1626	2.2	0.0234	0.6	0.0116	0.3
Household Characteristics	Ln Household Expenditure	0.0149	0.3	0.0259	0.6	-0.0176	-0.6	-0.0011	0.0
	Access to Piped Water	0.0101	0.2	-0.2250	-2.4	-0.0884	-1.7	-0.0701	-1.2
	Household Size	-0.0029	-0.4	0.0001	0.0	0.0030	0.6	0.0064	1.6
	Number of Children Aged 0-4	-0.0123	-0.5	-0.0082	-0.3	0.0451	2.7	0.0203	1.3
	Number of Children Aged 5-14	0.0315	1.7	0.0190	0.8	-0.0021	-0.2	-0.0274	-2.0
	Male Household Head	0.1573	2.2	-0.0600	-0.6	-0.0794	-1.7	0.0641	1.5
Local Labor Market Variables	Labor Demand**	1.9848	5.5	1.7388	3.8	1.5247	7.0	1.4460	6.8
	Labor Supply***	1.1748	2.7	0.3322	0.8	0.0528	0.2	-0.0233	-0.1

Source: UCW calculations based on the Gambia Joint Rural Labour Force/CDDP Baseline Survey, 2008.
Note: * The higher education category includes vocational postsecondary schools, colleges, post O-Level vocational and technical schools, universities, and master and PhD. programs. ** Labor demand is proxied by the prime age employment to population ratio. *** Labor supply is proxied by the youth to prime age population ratio.

Appendix Table B.8: Marginal Youth Employment Probability Effects, for Rural Areas, by Level of Education, 2008 RY

Explanatory variables		No Schooling		Primary		Secondary		Higher*	
		dy/dx	z	dy/dx	Z	dy/dx	z	dy/dx	z
Youth Age and Gender	Age	0.1223	2.0	0.4347	2.9	0.0533	0.4	-0.0016	0.0
	Age Squared	-0.0030	-1.9	-0.0104	-2.7	-0.0003	-0.1	0.0007	0.1
	Male	-0.0043	-0.2	0.0924	1.6	0.2044	4.3	0.0809	1.2
Household Characteristics	Ln Household Expenditure	-0.0175	-1.0	0.0018	0.0	-0.1268	-3.1	-0.1276	-2.3
	Access to Piped Water	-0.0172	-0.6	-0.0066	-0.1	-0.0756	-1.4	-0.0930	-1.2
	Household Size	0.0112	3.5	0.0008	0.1	0.0081	1.2	0.0147	1.3
	Number of Children Aged 0-4	0.0114	1.3	0.0292	1.2	0.0609	2.7	-0.0481	-1.2
	Number of Children Aged 5-14	-0.0079	-1.2	-0.0025	-0.1	0.0097	0.6	0.0056	0.3
	Male Household Head	0.0672	1.0	-0.0049	-0.1	-0.1108	-1.6	0.1781	1.7
Local Labor Market Variables	Labor Demand**	1.5184	10.1	4.0053	9.0	3.6820	7.6	3.3822	6.0
	Labor Supply***	0.0461	0.3	1.2446	3.0	1.3298	3.4	0.8138	1.2

Source: UCW calculations based on the Gambia Joint Rural Labour Force/CDDP Baseline Survey, 2008.
Note: * The higher education category includes vocational postsecondary schools, colleges, post O-Level vocational and technical schools, universities, and master and PhD. programs. ** Labor demand is proxied by the prime age employment to population ratio. *** Labor supply is proxied by the youth to prime age population ratio.

Appendix C: Children's Work and Child Labor

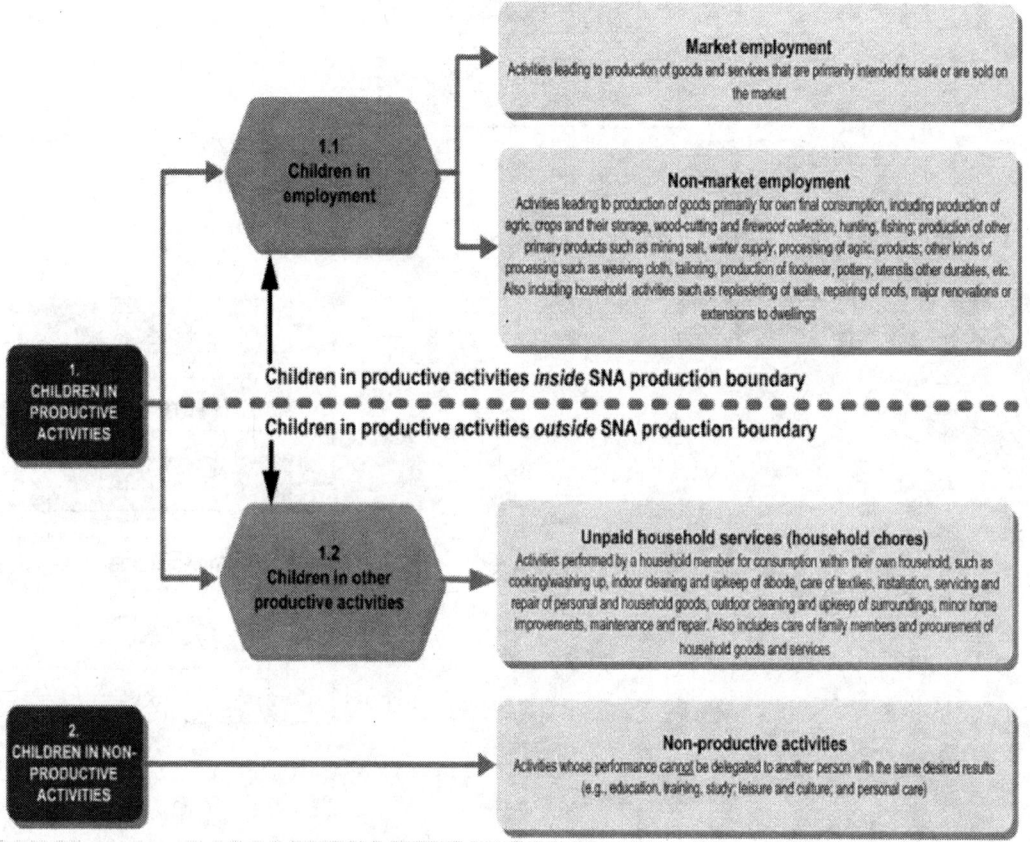

Market employment
Activities leading to production of goods and services that are primarily intended for sale or are sold on the market

1.1 Children in employment

Non-market employment
Activities leading to production of goods primarily for own final consumption, including production of agric. crops and their storage, wood-cutting and firewood collection, hunting, fishing; production of other primary products such as mining salt, water supply; processing of agric. products; other kinds of processing such as weaving cloth, tailoring, production of footwear, pottery, utensils other durables, etc. Also including household activities such as replastering of walls, repairing of roofs, major renovations or extensions to dwellings

1. CHILDREN IN PRODUCTIVE ACTIVITIES

Children in productive activities *inside* SNA production boundary
Children in productive activities *outside* SNA production boundary

1.2 Children in other productive activities

Unpaid household services (household chores)
Activities performed by a household member for consumption within their own household, such as cooking/washing up, indoor cleaning and upkeep of abode, care of textiles, installation, servicing and repair of personal and household goods, outdoor cleaning and upkeep of surroundings, minor home improvements, maintenance and repair. Also includes care of family members and procurement of household goods and services

2. CHILDREN IN NON-PRODUCTIVE ACTIVITIES

Non-productive activities
Activities whose performance cannot be delegated to another person with the same desired results (e.g., education, training, study; leisure and culture; and personal care)

Appendix D: Organizational Structure of the GTTI

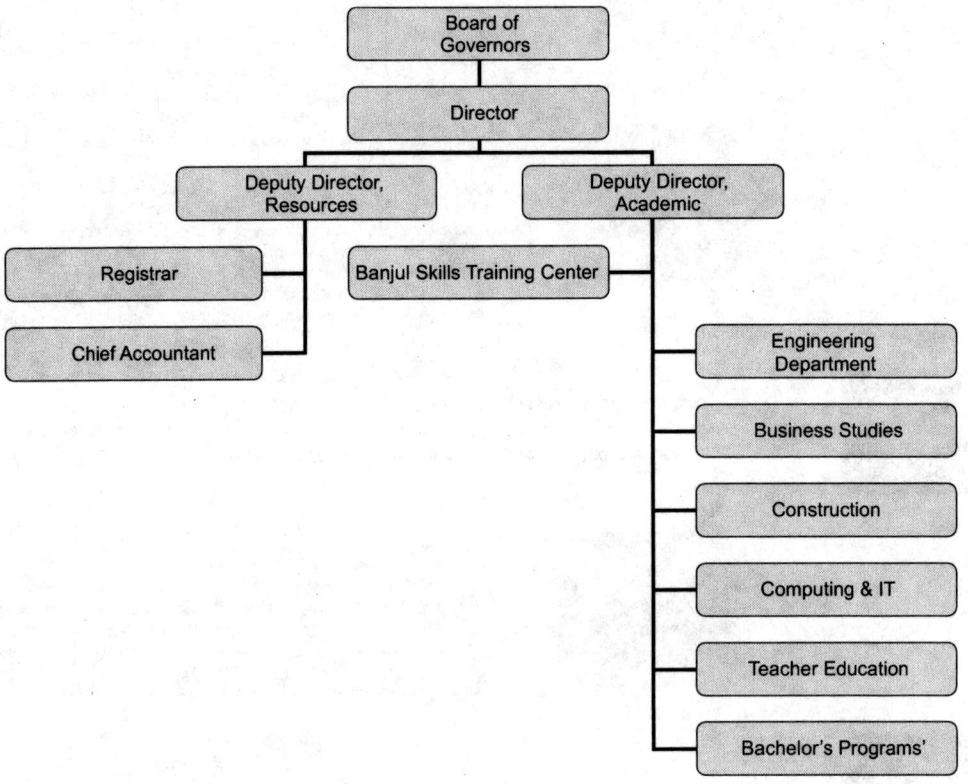

Source: GTTI.

Appendix E: Training Needs Assessment
Examination of the Scarcity of Skills

The National Training Authority (NTA) has conducted two types of training needs assessment: a household survey in 2006 and an enterprise survey in 2007. These surveys provided the basis to identify skills most in demand. The enterprise survey covered 338 enterprises over the 13 main categories of economic activity. Just over half were in wholesale and retail trade, 12 percent were in community and social services, and 12 percent were hotels, restaurants, and bars. Manufacturing accounted for just 4.1 percent of firms surveyed, construction for 3.3 percent and transport for 2.7 percent.

Given this profile, most paid employees were managers, salespeople, accountants, and secretaries. Skills in short supply were especially related to the wholesale and retail trades, namely: marketing (18.4 percent), management (9.6 percent), and business (6.7 percent). Traditional vocational trades, as a group, amounted to a significant 41 percent of the scarce skills.[1] Eleven percent responded that no skill was difficult to find in the labor market. The scarcity of skills varied considerably by area of economic activity, as shown below:

Appendix Table E.1: Selected Scarce Skills, by Sector (percent)

	Trade	Services	Hotels	Transport	Communi- cations	Manufac- turing	Construc- tion
Marketing	25.6	13.5	—	—	—	—	—
Management	16.6	—	12.8	—	16.7	—	—
Computing & IT	—	10.8	—	—	50.0	—	—
Technical	—	10.8	—	11.1		—	—
Carpentry & Construction	—	—	12.8	—	—	—	11.1
Cooking	—	—	12.8	—	—	—	—
Electrical	—	—	10.3	—	—	25.0	—
Engineering	—	—	—	22.2	—	—	—
Accounting	—	—	—	—	16.7	—	—
Mechanical	—	—	—	—	—	16.7	22.2
Technician	—	—	—	—	—	41.7	11.1

Source: NTA Enterprise Survey, 2007.

Some of the definitions of occupational categories are ambiguous, including "technical," "engineering" and "technician." These require further clarification. In addition, the survey report did not indicate the number of vacancies as a percentage of employment in the various economic sectors, which would be helpful.

In the household survey, employed persons identified the following kinds of skill needs:

Appendix Table E.2: Perceived Skill Needs of the Employed (percent)

Rank	Skill	Male	Female	Total
1	Tailoring/Designing/Sewing	6.9	18.6	12.9
2	Welding and Fabrication	11.4	5.2	8.2
3	Tie & Dye	1.5	12.8	7.3
4	Plumber	8.6	4.5	6.5
5	Mechanic	8.4	3.2	5.7
6	Carpenter/Carpentry	7.3	4.1	5.6
7	Electrician	6.4	3.3	4.8
8	Technician	4.3	3.1	3.7
9	Hair dresser	0.4	5.2	2.9
10	Mason	3.4	1.4	2.4
11	Business - Management Training	1.7	2.5	2.1
12	Computer	2.2	1.5	1.8
13	Soap making	0.3	2.8	1.6
	Nothing missing	20.6	20.7	20.7

Source: Household Survey, Selected Data from Table 6.

Appendix Table E.3: Perceived Further Training Needs, by Gender (percentage of the labor force)

Rank	Men		Women	
1	Business	9.1	Tie & Dye	19.8
2	Computer	6.2	Business	12.2
3	Mechanic	5.2	Tailoring/Sewing and Design	10.2
4	Carpentry	5.1	Soap Making	8.9
5	Welding	3.9	Gardening/Farming	7.1
6	Gardening/Farming	3.2	Computer	6.5
7	Driving	2.6	Accounting	1.7
8	Tailoring/Sewing and Design	2.6	Hairdressing	0.9
9	Construction	2.3	(Petty) Trading	0.7
10	Plumbing	2.2	Hotel Training	0.7
11	Accounting	1.8	Nursing	0.7
12	Teaching	1.7	Cooking	0.7
13	Electrician	1.5	Teaching	0.6
14	Management	1.7	Typing	0.6
15	Masonry	1.3	Management	0.6
	No Training Needed	31.1	No Training Needed	19.3
	Missing	5.4	Missing	3.7

Source: Household Survey, 2006.

The NTA carried out further interviews with manufacturing companies to determine skills in demand and found disparities between the engineering skills taught at the GTTI and those needed in the workplace, such as the ability of engineering students to read technical drawings.[2]

Employees' Education and Training

The Gambia Investment Climate Assessment (ICA) results show the constraints perceived by firms at the time of the survey in terms of skills, while comparing The Gambia's performance with some other countries in the region and other middle income countries. In The Gambia, firms in the manufacturing sector appear to be more concerned about the quality of the education of their workforce (15.2 percent) than other formal sector firms (10.6 percent for services, 11.8 percent for the informal sector, and 10.6 percent for the others).

From a cross-country perspective, middle-income countries such as Brazil (39 percent) and South Africa (35 percent) are more likely to report being limited by inadequate skills and labor regulations than the poorer countries in Sub-Saharan Africa. The Gambia is still highly dependent on large shares of agriculture and informal sector employment, which are typically intensive in nonskilled workers. Middle-income countries, on the other hand, have increased their medium-technology manufacturing sector and their rate of capital accumulation.

The rigidity of employment is 20 percent lower in The Gambia than the average for Sub-Saharan Africa. This may imply that employment procedures are simple and that there are few limitations in terms of hiring, working hours or retrenchment procedures. According to the 2006 ICA, this assumption should be handled with caution as it may be that firms only declare a small fraction of their workforce to the administration, which could point to problems with labor regulations, that should not be neglected.

Besides an inadequately educated workforce, other factors lead to significant investment constraints, such as the willingness to work for lower wages, and work discipline and attitudes. To the extent that available workers lack the skills employers need, unemployment would be "structural"—that is, a mismatch between job requirements and available skills. However unemployment in The Gambia is mostly "cyclical"—that is, the inability of the economy to create sufficient paid jobs. This means that most youth entering the labor market will have to work in the informal sector, probably being self-employed. Skills development can help create production capacities, including for self-employment. However, it is only one element of the equation. Alone, it is not the panacea for unemployment problems.

The ICA includes individual interviews of about 120 employees from the manufacturing sector, 59 of which were aged 15 to 24 years at the time of employment. The following graph presents the education levels of the formal sector employees in the manufacturing sector in The Gambia. Cross-country comparisons are made possible by a range of enterprise surveys used in ICA reports (see Figure E.1).

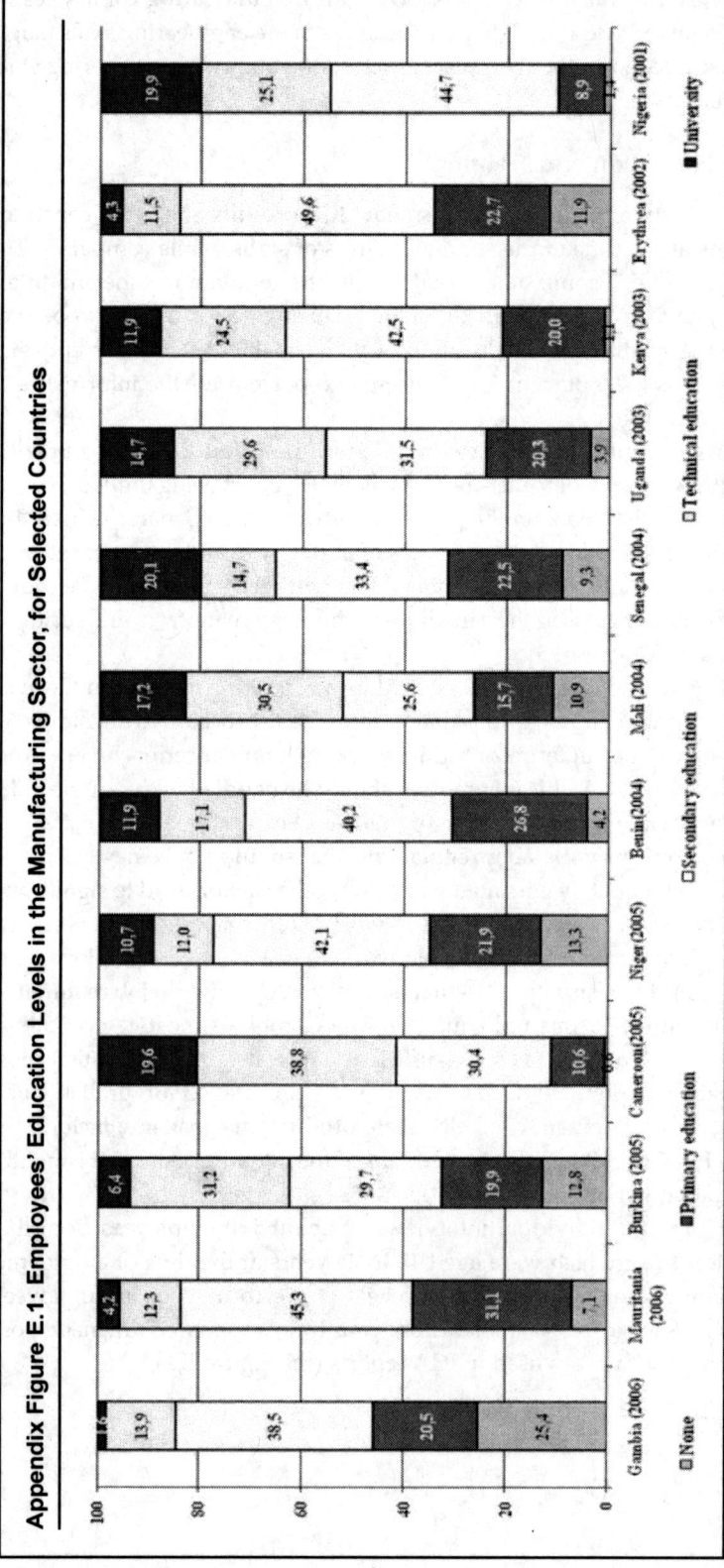

Appendix Figure E.1: Employees' Education Levels in the Manufacturing Sector, for Selected Countries

Source: Based on the employee questionnaire results of the Enterprise Survey, 2006.
Note: Exclusively for manufacturing firms.

The figure compares the proportions of manufacturing sector employees who achieved a given education level across select African countries for which data was available.[3] The data suggest that a large part of the manufacturing workforce (38.5 percent) has achieved secondary education. However, The Gambia has an extremely large proportion of employees with no education (25.4 percent), far above what is observed in even the worst such cases, namely Burkina Faso and Niger. The Gambia also has one of the lowest proportions of employees with technical education (13.9 percent) and university degrees.

Other data indicate that gender differences in education levels persist. Although more women have primary level education, they are underrepresented at higher educational levels and even absent at the university level.

In a situation where almost half the workforce has received only primary education or none at all, and where technical and university education are underdeveloped, professional training provided by firms to their employees is a key contribution to the improvement of workers' qualifications and productivity. According to the data, almost a quarter of manufacturing firms in The Gambia provides formal training to their employees. This is low compared with Mali and Senegal, and very low compared with countries like China or Brazil.

The proportion of employees receiving formal training varies across sectors, from zero in the garments sector, to 48 percent for other manufacturing firms and almost 70 percent in the food and beverage industry. The proportion of employees benefiting from formal training in the manufacturing sector also varies according to the size of firms and their ownership: foreign owned firms tend to rely more on formal training than national ones. Production workers are those who most benefit from training.

Notes

1. Including technical (9.3 percent), carpentry and construction (8.7 percent), electrical (7.6 percent), mechanical (6.7 percent), engineering (3.5 percent), cooking (1.7 percent) and welding (1.7 percent).
2. NTA, Shortages of Skilled Workers in the Manufacturing Sector.
3. The comparison is made on the basis of the employee questionnaire that manufacturing sector workers responded to. These questionnaires are only available in enterprise surveys carried out in Africa. Therefore, the comparators are different from those mentioned in the rest of the report and pertain exclusively to Sub-Saharan Africa.

Appendix F: The NTA's Functional Structure

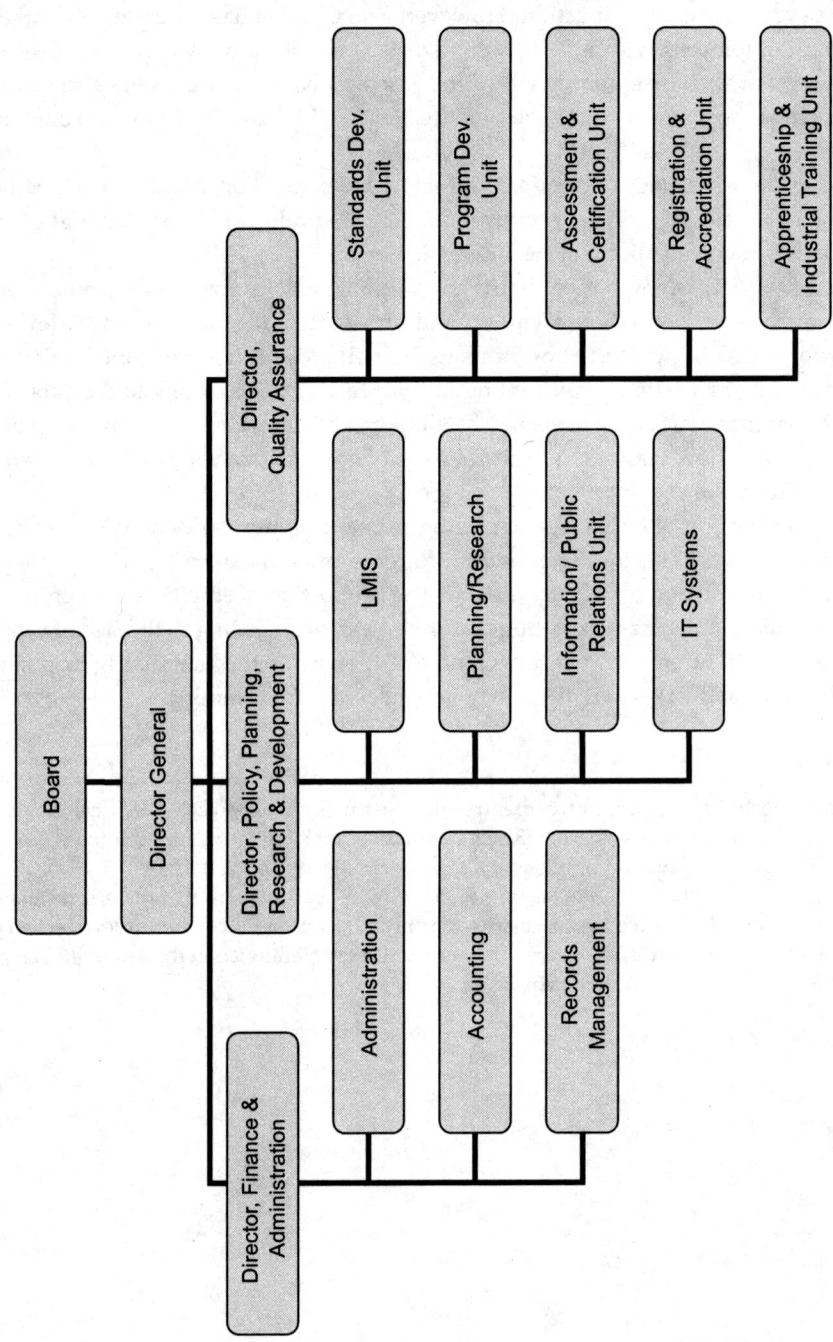

Appendix G: Experience with Training Funds in World Bank-Financed Projects in Sub-Saharan Africa[1]

Overview

The experience with training funds has been generally positive in both the formal and informal sectors. Two funds even began to cross subsidize training in the informal sector, that is, allocate funds raised from levies on the formal sector to finance informal sector training. The development of training funds requires painstaking preparation, including agreements at high policy levels on their rationale, purpose, and benefits. Good management and financial autonomy seem to be essential requirements for effectiveness. Balance in the governance structure of a fund is also clearly important; tripartite structures often work well provided that employers have a major voice. Finally, linking training funds with national training authorities seems to work well: the presence of funds can make a training authority more effective, and the authority can help target the use of funds better.

Findings

The World Bank policy study on skills development[2] recommended the establishment of training funds as sources of targeted financial assistance to employers and training institutions "to increase flexibility in responding to periodic training needs..." During the 1990s, nine countries created or supported training funds of various types to finance training provision in high priority areas.[3] The purported advantage of these funds was the ability to finance specific targeted training based on surveys of needs or proposals by beneficiaries. Typically, the funds also had the ability to generate competition among training providers by making all institutions that met minimum standards eligible to receive funds. The underlying aim was to change incentives for existing training institutions and stimulate a supply response to market forces. In addition to increasing resources for TVET, funds can also make it possible to involve nongovernmental stakeholders in the control of funds to which they have contributed.

Experiences with training funds have generally been positive:

- The *Madagascar* project successfully provided training both to the formal and informal sectors;
- The *Côte d'Ivoire* project helped unify two levies under the Labor Force Training Support Project (FDFP). Two main institutional factors account for its success, namely: (i) its autonomous structure, and (ii) the direct transfer of payroll taxes from the treasury to the training agency. The FDFP has even begun to cross subsidize training in the informal sector. This is highly unusual. The cross subsidization by FDFP amounts to 18 to 20 percent of the training allocations (that are not Bank financed);
- The training fund in *Mauritius* also appears to be successful, benefiting from a growing economy, that made the Industrial and Vocational Training Board less dependent on external financing. The economy was so buoyant that reserves accumulated in the fund and eventually led to reductions in the relative fund income. The fund's performance could reportedly have been improved if the appraisal criteria for subprojects had been better developed;

▓   *Mauritania's* experience is instructive because it included two funds, one successful and the other not. The Institutional Support Fund was intended to finance the development and delivery of training courses by TVET institutions in response to employer requests, in effect extending the range of services provided by these institutions. At project completion only a dozen projects had been financed and only a quarter of available funds had been disbursed. Factors responsible include (i) delays in legally enabling the institutions to use the funds, (ii) a restrictive operational manual and a complicated evaluation process, and (iii) insufficient public awareness of the fund's existence. In contrast, the Training Support Fund was successful in financing training activities initiated by microenterprises. More than 130 proposals were financed, generated by groups of workers and cooperatives. The results reportedly enabled the beneficiary microenterprises to become more productive. The demand-driven nature of initiatives supported by the TSF, facilitated by participation of microenterprises in the design of the program, was reportedly easily implemented and had a substantial impact. Still, the fund was able to use only three quarters of available funds because of the initial lack of clarity in procedures for accessing the financing; and

▓   The smaller training funds in the *Cape Verde* projects also appear to be functioning successfully.

Several observations can be made about training funds:

▓   The successes supported by World Bank financing over the past decade should not obscure the difficulties in making training funds effective: the administrative requirements are complex; and financial sustainability depends not only on a steady and secure source of financing, but also how the funds are received. The best alternative appears to be directly from the Treasury, as in Côte d'Ivoire, but this is frequently challenged. Endowments may be another way to ensure steady and secure funding;

▓   The Togo case shows that the establishment of a training fund is a very demanding task that requires painstaking preparation. Agreements need to be sought from the highest levels about the rationale, purpose and benefits of the fund;

▓   Good management and financial autonomy seem to be essential requirements for effectiveness. Both of these characteristics apply to the FDFP in Côte d'Ivoire. In Madagascar, the structure of the Centre National de la Fonction Publique Territoriale (CNFTP) as a semi-autonomous body contributed greatly to its ultimate effectiveness;

▓   Balance in a fund's governance structure is important. Governance in Côte d'Ivoire's FDFP was balanced between government, employers, and workers. This mix was highly effective. It prevented one party from dominating and distorting the operations of the Fund. The opposite was true in the Togo project, where the Minister of Vocational Education and Training had a too powerful influence in operations;

▓   Linking training funds with training councils seems to work well. The presence of funds can make an advisory council more effective, and the council can help target the use of funds better. This combination worked particularly well in Madagascar; and

■ Clear, straightforward (meaning not overly complex) procedures for approval of fund allocations are essential, as shown in the Madagascar and Mauritania cases.

Notes

1. Adapted from Johanson, 2006.
2. Middleton et al., 1993.
3. Benin (FODEFCA), Cape Verde (Basic Education and Training Support Fund), Comoros (Vocational Training Fund), Côte d'Ivoire (Labor Force Training Support Project, FDFP), Madagascar (Centre National de la Fonction Publique Territoriale—CNFTP), Mali (Vocational Training Support Fund), Mauritius, Mauritania (Institutional Support Fund and the Training Support Fund), and Togo (National Training Fund).

Appendix H: Terms of Reference for the Study to Redesign the Training Levy

Background

Reforms in the financing of skills development have been problematic and leave an important gap in the system. The second prong of the TVET policy and strategy was the financial framework—the training levy. The plan was to introduce a training levy based on 0.25 percent of annual revenue (turnover) of enterprises. This was applied in 2007 but only lasted one month in implementation. Enterprises with high turnover and low profit margins (such as commercial banks) petitioned the President in the first month of the levy operation (January 2007) and he rescinded the Act. In its place the levy reverted to a historical schedule, with firms over D 5 million paying D 50,000 a year, and those under paying D 30,000. Even this formula is flawed, as smaller firms are not exempt and many complain they cannot pay the D 30,000 levy as it would take an excessive share their meager profits.

The levy system needs to be studied and redesigned as a matter of priority so that one can be introduced that has both the capacity to generate sufficient revenue and has the support of employers.

Scope of Work

1. Training Levy

Overall, the consultant will take into account prior studies on training levies in The Gambia and international experience in the implementation of training levies, will outline options, assess the options, and make specific recommendations on revision of the training levy.

The main questions to be answered are:

- Does a training levy make good economic sense in The Gambia?
- What should be the objectives of a revised training levy?
- What type of levy mechanism would best meet the objectives?
- What key success conditions must be included in revision of the levy system, for example consultation and consensus with employers?
- What level of resources would a revised levy mechanism likely raise?
- What specific conditions are required to make the levy system administratively feasible?
- How can a revised levy be implemented?

Specific tasks include the following:

- Identify essential objectives for a revised training levy, including provision of incentives for employers to provide in-service training of workers; mobilization of resources to expand the supply of pertinent skills and establishment/expansion of a training market.
- Establish a basis for levy payments (including rationale, sources, rate, exemptions for size or type of firm) appropriate for the objectives

- Ensure minimum administrative burden on collection and administering of funds
- Specific issue: whether government agencies would pay the levy
- Make rough projection of likely revenue from a revised training levy under different methods and rates

- Determine collection agency and methods—to maximize compliance and keep administrative costs to a minimum.
- Work out the administrative and staffing implications of the levy options
- Identify implementation requirements and sequencing for revision of the levy, including identification of potential obstacles and strategies to overcome them.
- Ascertain views of the key stakeholders on various options, especially employers and the GCCI
- Conduct a (series of) final presentation(s) of options and recommendations as a basis for decisions.

2. Other VET Financing Matters

In addition, the consultant will:

- Advise generally on ways to mobilizing resources outside the levy system for expanding skills development and meeting critical skills shortages;
- Recommend how the government's own funds should be administered through the National Training Authority;
- Advise on methods of normative financing for allocation of resources for skills development through the NTA.
- Advise on ways the government can encourage non government training providers, including NGOs engaged in training

Outputs and Deliverables

- Presentation of options and recommendations at workshop (Powerpoint)
- Draft report covering the above topics, taking into account comments received from stakeholders at the final workshops
- Final report, taking into account comments received from the Bank, government, NTA and other stakeholders.

Modus Operandi

The consultant will work closely with the National Training Authority—which will arrange meetings and provide logistical support—and the Project Coordination Office of the World Bank.

References

Adams, A.V. 2007. "The Role of Youth Skills Development in the Transition to Work: A Global Review." World Bank, Human Development Network Children and Youth Department, Series 5.

Bosworth, B. P. and S. M. Collins. 2003. "The Empirics of growth: An Update." Brookings Papers on Economic Activity, no. 2.

Castro, C. 1999. "Proyecto Joven: New Solutions and Some Surprises, Inter-American Development Bank." Washington, D.C.

Castro, C. and Verdisco, A. 1998. "Training Unemployed Youth in Latin America: Same Old Sad Story?" Inter-American Development Bank, Washington, D.C.

Cigno, R. and Z. Tzannatos. 2002. "Child Labour Handbook."

Deb, P. and F. Rosati. 2002. "Determinants of Child Labour and School Attendance: the Role of Household Observables."

Docquier, F. and A. Marfouk. 2006. "International Migration by Educational Attainment (1990-2000)." in Ozden, C. and M. Schiff (eds.), "International Migration, Remittances and the Brain Drain." Chapter 5.

Docquier, F. and K. Sekkat. 2006. "The Brain Drain: What Do We Know?" Research report prepared for the AFD, Paris.

Docquier, F. 2006. "Brain Drain and Inequality across Nations." Paper presented at the EUDN-AFD conference on migration and development, Paris, November 8.

Dougherty, C. and J. P. Tan. 1989. "The Cost Effectiveness of National Training Systems in Developing Countries." World Bank, Population and Human Resources Department, Washington, D.C.

Dumont, J-C. and G. Dumaître. 2005. "Counting Immigrants and Expatriates in OECD Countries: A New Perspective." OECD Social, Employment and Migration Working Paper n°25-39.

Government of The Gambia. 1996. "Vision 2020."

GTTI (The Gambia Technical Training Institute). 2001. "Report for the 2000/01 Academic Year."

Guarcello, L., S. Lyon and F. Rosati. 2006. "Child Labour and Education for All: An Issue Paper." UCW (Understanding Children's Work) Working Paper No. 19.

Guarcello, L., S. Lyon and F. Rosati. 2006. "The Twin Challenges of Child labour and Youth Employment in Ethiopia." UCW (Understanding Children's Work) Working Paper No. 18.

Gubert, F. and C. J. Nordman. 2006. "Migration from MENA to OECD Countries: Trends, Determinants and Prospects." Background Paper for World Bank, MENA Department, Washington, D.C.

Hanushek, E. A. and L. Woessman. 2007. "The Role of Education Quality in Economic Growth." World Bank Policy Research Working Paper No. 4122, February.

Heckman, J. 1979. "Sample Selection Bias as a Specification Error." *Econometrica*, No. 47.

ICA (Investment Climate Assessment of The Gambia). 2006. World Bank, Africa Region, Private Sector and Finance Unit.

ICA (Investment Climate Assessment of The Gambia). 2009. World Bank, Africa Region, Private Sector and Finance Unit.

ILO (International Labour Office). 2006. "The End of Child Labour: Within Reach." Geneva.

Johanson, R. K. and A. V. Adams. 2006. "Skills Development in Sub-Saharan Africa."

Johanson, R. K. 2002. "Sub-Saharan Africa: Regional Response to Bank TVET Policy in the 1990s." African Federation for Technology in Health Care 4. World Bank. Washington, D.C.

"Joint World Bank and African Development Country Assistance Strategy." 2008. Report No. 42267-GM, February 1.

Middleton, J., A. Van Adams and A. Ziderman. 1993. "Skills for Productivity: Vocational Education and Training in Developing Countries." World Bank, Oxford University Press.

Mincer J. 1974. "Schooling, Experience and Earnings." National Bureau of Economic Research. Cambridge Massachusetts.

Mitchell, J., and J. Faal. 2008. "The Gambian Tourist Value Chain and Prospects for Pro-Poor Tourism." ODI (Overseas Development Institute) Working Paper No. 289, March.

NTA (National Training Authority). 2007. "Shortages of Skilled Workers in the Manufacturing Industry." Draft document.

NTA (National Training Authority). 2007. "Training Needs Assessment, Enterprise Survey."

"Public Expenditure Review." 2006. Prepared by Emanic Consulting.

SIMI (Sahel Investment Management International) Ltd. 2003. "Review of the Gambia Technical Training Institute's Development Plan for 1999-2002 and Formulation of a New Plan for 2002-2006." Consultancy Final Report, Banjul, August.

Soh, H. 2009. "Poverty Assessment." World Bank, Africa Region.

"The Gambia Integrated Household Survey on Consumption Expenditure." 2003.

Tuck, R. 2007. "An Introductory Guide to National Qualifications Frameworks: Conceptual and Practical Issues for Policy Makers." ILO (International Labor Office), Skills and Employability Department, Geneva.

Young, M. 2005. "National Qualification Frameworks: Their Feasibility for Effective Implementation in Developing Countries." ILO (International Labor Office), Skills Working Paper No. 22, Geneva.

ECO-AUDIT
Environmental Benefits Statement

The World Bank is committed to preserving endangered forests and natural resources. The Office of the Publisher has chosen to print World Bank Studies and Working Papers on recycled paper with 30 percent postconsumer fiber in accordance with the recommended standards for paper usage set by the Green Press Initiative, a non-profit program supporting publishers in using fiber that is not sourced from endangered forests. For more information, visit www.greenpressinitiative.org.

In 2009, the printing of these books on recycled paper saved the following:
- 289 trees*
- 92 million Btu of total energy
- 27,396 lb. of net greenhouse gases
- 131,944 gal. of waste water
- 8,011 lb. of solid waste

*40 feet in height and 6–8 inches in diameter

green
press
INITIATIVE